"This Ain't No Self Help Book: Motivation for a Modern Age"

By
Jack A. Terry

"This Ain't No Self Help Book: Motivation for a Modern Age"
By
Jack A. Terry

Table of Contents

Introduction, part one

Hey you.

Yeah, you right there. You finally picked a book, maybe off a shelf, maybe online, maybe from the discount bin, and decided to read more than the back cover. If you're like most people, you've probably dipped your big toe into a few different books, trying to figure out if the author seems trustworthy, honest, human. Maybe this isn't even the first introduction you've read. You had another book in mind, you read a couple of pages, you said "Hmmmm, maybe, but I just don't know." Maybe it sounded like it was good, but just not right for you. Trust me, I know your pain.

I do the same thing. I'll stand in front of a row of books and I'll look at all those titles and all I want is one that just calls out to me, one that says "Pick me! I'm the one you want!" I look at one or another, flip through it and maybe read a couple of pages, but almost always I would put them back up on the shelf, something just not being right, and most of the time I would leave empty handed. You might too. (Granted, I hope not, but anyway…) I do the same thing with cookbooks, specifically diet cookbooks, trying to find the right one for me, paranoid that if I choose the wrong one, not only will I not follow the regimen, but that it will be detrimental to me in the end. (On the other hand, I can buy a piece of fiction without thinking twice about it. Pretty picture on the cover? Clever title? Yeah, that's usually good enough for me. But we're not here to talk about me. We're here to talk about you.)

Now, I can't tell you if this book is any better than any other book you've come across. I probably can't even tell you what other books are even out there. The problem with books like this is that they multiply quicker than rabbits. Everybody's got a story to tell and think that it's worth hearing. Hubris or wisdom? You decide. I wouldn't be surprised if, in the time it's taken you to read this far, two new titles were published. I don't know if my book is better, or worse, or more insightful or practical or pragmatic or more anything. It is what it is. Later on in this book I'll talk about why there are better ways to measure things than by comparing them to others, but in the meantime I'll tell you why mine is different from the rest.

This ain't no self help book.

Curious now?

Yeah, I know what you're thinking. You want to call "shenanigans" on me. If it isn't a self help book, what's it doing on a shelf full of other self help books under a sign that says "self help books"? You might even be on a self help book webpage for all I know. But it isn't, I swear. It's better.

Look, you've come this far. I need you to come a little bit farther. I want you to take this book and get comfortable. If you're in a store, and the store is anything like the stores I shop in, there are some overstuffed chairs to sit in, or at least a rolling foot stool in an aisle for the short people to get the books on the top shelves. Take a seat, relax, and stay with me. And don't panic. I used to always get uncomfortable, thinking everyone was looking at me, thinking "Yo, that dude must be crazy. Looking at him needing the self help." Well, let me first burst your bubble by telling you that there aren't that many, if any, people looking at you right now. And those that are, between you and me, probably need more help than both of us. In fact, my guess is that they're even a little jealous of you and your bravery to take the first step. So let's take the second step and have a seat.

Comfy? Good.

There are many reasons why I say that this isn't a self help book. First of all, to me the phrase "self help" implies that everything is being done in a vacuum, with no outside help. That simply isn't possible. We are, for better or worse, who we are because of the way other people and their thoughts and behaviors have influenced and shaped us, and we will become the people we want to be with the help of those that are in our lives now. You may think you don't need anyone's help. You might not even want anyone's help because you feel a stigma attached to making changes in your life. The short answer now is you're going to need their help. The long answer, concerning how to ask for and accept that help, and how to recognize good help from bad, comes later, but for the meantime, simply understand that you don't do anything in this world on your own.

The second reason is that "self help" books tend to almost always have a plan they expect you to follow. "Follow these easy steps," they say, or "These are the five things you need to know." Just look at some of the other titles. I'll tell you right now, if there is a number in the title, there are that many steps inside to follow. Now, far be it from me to say this is a bad thing. Before this book is over, I'll certainly tell you a couple of things I think you should do. And you might be something who looks for the structure and who needs it to help you on your journey. This book in your hand will not work for everyone, and every book on the shelf will not work for you. My point simply is that this book isn't an instruction manual. It is as much a memoir and a work of philosophy as it is intended to be helpful. As far as philosophy goes, I don't think it's going to challenge the whole "God is dead/I think, therefore I am" branch of philosophy, but it is a book concerning a lifestyle, one that I have lived, one I am living now, and the absolute joy of trying to tie them together. (If ever something sounds like it might be sarcastic, it probably is meant to be. Intonation is hard to get across in written form, so I'll just throw out right now that I tend to be just a bit sarcastic. Trust me.) Writing this book helps me keep track of my life, and to make sure I am learning from it, as I try to go from practicing at life to being in life the person I know myself to be. Are there lessons to be learned in here? Of course, but there are probably also lessons to be learned from People Magazine too, if you read it right. Some of this book will be insights into things I've learned, some will be stories of things I've done. All of it is designed to help you be the person you want to be.

Finally, there is one last reason why calling this book a "self-help" book would be misleading. In truth, it is a self help book. For me. I didn't write this for you. (I know that's going to do wonders for prying that $19.95 out of your wallet.) I wrote it for me, in fits and starts, for as many reasons as there are sections in it, but all for one purpose: To not forget. Through everything I've experienced, both the highs and lows, there have been lessons I have learned that have helped make me a better person. Some of those lessons were painful ones. Some were not even things I realized I needed to learn until long after the fact, but all of them are important. The reason the pen first met the paper about any of it was because I knew it was important for me to remember; that it would come back to be important for me to know.

And just like the pen meets the paper, now it's time for the rubber to meet the road. I know you're comfortable, but it's time to get up, walk to the counter, hand the nice person behind the counter some money (or a credit card, or a debit card, or a gift card, or a personal check, or whatever else passes for currency these days) and take me home. I've got so much more to talk to you about.

Introduction, part two.

Nice House.

So, you bought the book, you brought it home, you did whatever you needed to do and now, here you are, perched in your favorite reading space. Could be a big winged back chair in a cozy den, could be propped up on five or six pillows in your bed. Could be outside somewhere, maybe in your garden. And who knows why you even bought it? Maybe the intro spoke to you. Maybe you found it funny. Maybe you know me and you're doing me a favor. (Thanks.) Maybe your spouse walked up to you and said "Are you ready?" and you were caught off guard and next thing you know you're buying it without necessarily wanting to. Whatever. You're here and I'm here with you.

As the words say at the top of the page, there is a little more I want to cover before we get started. I know, I know, you want to jump right into the good stuff. You're no different than the rest of us. Think of this as the cooling off time before eating and swimming. You read the first part and it filled you up. Now, you need to digest that before you start doing cannonballs off the high dive. Trust me; the swimming pool ain't going anywhere.

Now that you got the book, one of three things is going to happen. Possibility *one* is that you are going to sit right here, where you are, and devour the book in one sitting. You are going to read it (and into it) for every possible morsel of truth and light and understanding that might be there, and when you are done, you will put the book down with authority. There will be heavenly sunlight streaming in through the windows, a chorus of angels will serenade you, you will gather all of your brood together and you will say to them, in all seriousness, that you no longer want to be known by your given name, but rather, from now on, you are to be called Moonstar Firetree, and you will lead them all to enlightenment. You will start recycling that which isn't recyclable and composting that which can't be composted. You will eat nothing but berries, clouds and nectar while practicing a transcendental meditative yoga-like tai chi. The old you will be shed like a dress on prom night and the new you will be a beacon for the entire world to navigate by.

If this happens to you, call me. I'd really like to meet you.

Possibility *two* is that you will finish this introduction, maybe read another chapter, maybe not, and then put the book somewhere convenient for you to pick up on occasion. Maybe on the night stand, or the coffee table, possibly even on the toilet. It will be waiting for you to read a few pages at a time, randomly flipping through to whatever chapter the book opens to. You will eventually read the whole thing, but in no direct order, and you will glean from it what you will, some pages standing out more in your mind than others. Maybe something you read will make you say to yourself "That sounds good." Maybe some will make you say "That's not for me." And maybe some will be things you already recognize to be true about yourself. It'll become a quasi-reference book, kept somewhere between the take-out menu of a Chinese delivery place and the Sports Illustrated swimsuit issue.

This can happen to a few of you.

Possibility *three* is that when you finish the introduction, you will say to yourself, "What was I thinking? I don't really need this. All I really need is (choose one) a good night sleep/a good meal/a little more exercise/a night out/a new job/etc., etc., etc." And later, over dinner, your spouse, or date, or kid, or pet, or whoever you talk to at dinner will ask you about the book you bought, and you'll mumble something about, "I don't know. Some story from some punk know-it-all who thinks he has it all figured out." Later you will take this book and put it on the bookshelf, wonder if you kept the receipt, head up to bed, and forget you ever bought it. For a while.

Maybe it'll be a long while. Maybe you really will forget that you bought it and years later, when you least expect it, you'll find it. And when you least expect it, you'll find that you need it. Maybe whatever brought you to buy the book has come back a little bigger, a little stronger, and you find yourself a little more lost, a little more confused. Who knows? Maybe that'll happen even later today. Maybe you're at that point where you are looking for that guidance, to help you get ducks in a row. You want to hear about someone else, how they handle things, how they got through life. And I'm not talking life on the big screen. Let's get something straight right now. There are many things in my life I haven't done. Here is a partial list. I have never…

- Spent time in prison for a crime I didn't commit.
- Serve in the Armed Forces, much less in a wartime situation.
- Cured anything, other than a hangover.
- Been the David in a *David v. Goliath* lawsuit
- Traveled across the ocean in a kayak.
- Earned an enormous sum of money after being born dirt poor to sharecroppers.
- Accomplished any sort of athletic achievement that would make my parents proud.

(A little note on the last one. I do have a pretty impressive athletic achievement that, twenty plus years after the fact, people still talk about. It didn't make my parents proud then, and it doesn't now.)

In other words, I'm just another worker bee like the vast majority of people out there. I've worked some different jobs and lived some different places, but in the end, I ain't much different from anyone else. That's why you're reading this. To see how someone like you gets by. Maybe just buying the book has given you a little level of satisfaction, of knowing that you are doing the right thing, that you are taking the first step to finding some order in the chaos, and it's time for you isn't now, but later. That's okay, for now. But just like buying a gym membership makes you feel healthier, it doesn't actually help you until you start using it. What's important is that the book will be here when you are ready for it.

This will happen to most of you.

To my left as I write this there is my collection of books. It is a much more modest collection than I used to have to be sure, but try moving around a lot. You'll discover the more heavy boxes of books you have, the fewer people you'll be able to find that will offer to help you move. That being said there is any number of books in all styles of writing. I will pick one up haphazardly and flip through: reaffirming what it is that I have learned from that book. To give you an indication, on the middle shelf, starting from the left, there is a novel by Leonard Cohen, one by Anne Tyler, the Bible, a book by the Dalai Lama, "Little Popcorn"—the first book I ever read (and no, it wasn't last week either, smarty pants!) and "Faust" by Goethe. That's only six books out of maybe a couple hundred. That's my point. This book will be on your shelf when you are ready for it. That may be today, maybe even right now. Or it will be later. The important thing is that when you are ready, so will it be.

I asked you before, and I'll ask you again.

Curious now?

If so, let's go. If not, don't sweat it. I'll be waiting for you on the next page.

Coming to terms with some terms

There are some words that are important in dealing with issues of <u>change</u> and <u>growth</u>. What is most important when dealing with words is recognizing something very important about them: They rarely mean what we think they mean. Sometimes we make them more important than we should, other times we minimize too much, but almost always we let them, in some way, overwhelm us. Later in the book I'm going to talk about the difference between hearing and listening, and this is very much a concern of that. But before we get there, I want to make sure you understand what I'm talking about.

Probably the greatest example of a word that is universally misunderstood is the word *love*. That's a word that is both the most important one a person can hear and also the most casual adjective. You may say it all the time without thinking about it, describing parts of your life that don't truly warrant the use of the word. I mean, can you honestly remember every song that you "loved?" But when it comes to really using it, i.e. with that special someone you've been seeing for a while and letting them know how you feel, we all go through such a thorough routine of mental gymnastics even the East German judge will give us a 10. Are we really ready to say it? Do we think they're ready to hear it? Are they going to say it back? If they don't, is there someway we can take it back? Are we sure it's even what we feel, or are we just really, really excited and that seems like the best way to describe it? It is this huge heavy word that hangs over us, yet if a person is asked to describe what it feels like to be in love, they use terms like "light" and "freeing" and "unbelievable" and "wonderful". In other words, the opposite of what we feel right before we say the word for the first time and probably even for many subsequent times afterwards, especially if our significant other does not, in fact, say it back to us.

In the end it is just another word: one that means a lot more than most, but still just a word. In fact, if one was to just sit with that word in meditation, and get away from the baggage that has been

13

dumped on it by everything from previous relationships to the Hallmark corporation, and just let themselves learn what that word truly means to them, I'm willing to bet they would have a better understanding of when they should use it and who deserves to hear it. In doing so the people they share it with would hear it, and feel it, much more sincerely.

So, some words carry weight they don't need to. And to make sure that you are ready for how it is you want to be living your life, there are some words we need to start redefining, or maybe even eliminating, for you.

Regret

The biggest challenge anyone faces when they start working on making a change is having an understanding of their past. Makes sense, because it is obviously our past that has shaped and defined us up until this point in our lives. In order to grow we need to be able to move beyond the past. We have to work to establish a new way of living, drawing from what we have learned, but taking those lessons and bringing them to the here and now, the true present, and not going back to live with them when we first learned them. It isn't necessarily the past that is the issue, but the word that it inevitably gets partnered up with. To some degree, every story that a person tells about their past comes with a sense of longing, a certain "Boy, wasn't that a great time? Sure wish we could do it again" to it. If there were no emotional attachment to a story, we wouldn't share it with anyone because we wouldn't think it mattered. The problem is that a lot of our stories matter for all the wrong reasons.

1 a: to mourn the loss or death of b: to miss very much
2: to be very sorry for

So says Webster.com. Figure out which word it's for? Yeah, that right. It's *regret*, one of the biggest little words on the planet. The weight that word carries, the sincerity implied when one starts a sentence with the phrase "I regret that I. . ." fill in the blanks, gives

14

this word so much power, that it can truly alter the way you live your life forever, and that is why that word needs to be eliminated. Let's look at all three of those definitions, one at a time.

1a: "To mourn the loss or death of". This, to me, is a definition of the word I've never heard. I'm not sure if I even believe this one. The way I look at it is to replace the word with the definition and see if it makes sense. "I mourn the loss of my father." Works. "I regret the loss of my father." Doesn't work, and here's why. Regret is a verb, a word of action, but I can not regret something I did not do. Now, if I had killed my father, I could certainly see regretting that, but to choose to regret something I can't control seems a bit preposterous to me.

1b: "To miss very much". Once again, this is something I can not accept because of the action involved. I miss my dad very much, but seeing as I'm not the reason he's no longer here, how can I feel regret over his passing? There are many other words that describe much more accurately the emotion, none better than the words in the definition itself.

2: "To be very sorry for". Now we're at least getting somewhere, because this is the definition that we all know and love and that sends us to our shrinks. "I feel very sorry for" *this action* sounds an awful lot like "I regret" *this action*. "I did something that I am not proud of, I am sorry that I did it and I regret it." (Sounds like half the politicians I know.) In reality, it is just a different way to say I'm sorry, as if the person saying it is backing up the apology, that not only are they upset that it happened, but that they also wish they could take it back. But I'm not sure how correct that is. Let me ask you a few questions:

1) Is there something in your life that you are sorry for?
2) Do you regret doing it?
3) If you could take it back, would you?
4) Why?

Harsh last question I know, and there are probably a few examples out there of why something should be taken back if it could be, but let me first take you through the argument most people have, before introducing you to the short cut to it.

People will say "I wish I never did" whatever "because if I hadn't done that, my life would have turned out differently." You

15

better believe it would have. It's called the butterfly effect, and it's been a template for a Ray Bradbury short story, an Ashton Kucher movie and both a Simpsons *and* a Family Guy episode. Any little difference in your past will surely alter the course of your life, and that to me is the greatest reason to not wish to change your past.

My life is here, now. There is no telling who I would have become if any one of a zillion things in my life had gone just a bit differently, but it is with absolute certainty I can say that I wouldn't be who I am here, now. Maybe I'd be better off, maybe I'd be worse, that is debatable for as long as the stars are in the sky, but accepting that I can never know who the other me might have turned out to be, who better than to be who I am here, now?

Whether a person believes in fate or free will, whether they think they are here for a reason or just because of cosmic happenstance, the fact remains that this is the point of their life that they are in. So wishing the past to be different is of no use, because it can't be done. You can not change any part of the past, you can not correct it, you can not relive it, you can not rekindle it (trust me on that one), you can not replace it. It is what it will always be. Best you can do is learn from it.

Some people will disagree and say the best you can do about some parts of it is to forget it, but I disagree, for two reasons. First of all, in trying to forget it or deny it, I believe it only gives it strength to come back to you when you least expect it or can handle it in your life. Most things that a person would want to forget would be circumstances surrounding a traumatic event, but if they don't confront the feelings that it brings up, work through them, and come to some kind of understanding, those emotions will always be there waiting to sabotage the person. Secondly, if we forget what we've been through, how are we to learn from it? And that leads me to the short cut:

You can't change it, so don't cry about it.

One of my personal mottos is "It is better to light a candle than curse the darkness." Meaning if something is bothering you, do something about it, but don't just sit there and bitch about it. This is just another example of that. You can piss and moan all you want about something that happened in the past, but that isn't going to make that event disappear. Don't curse it; work on it. Make sure that you learn from it. Wasting your time wishing it were different will keep you living in the past and not the present.

Which brings me to my final thought about regret, for now anyway: Regret and sorrow are two different things. I am sorry for the way I have treated people, how I have hurt them, words that I said to them. I am sorry for some of my actions in life, and the results that they created. It was never my intention to create pain and havoc in other people's lives, and I accept that there is a certain level of selfishness in my beliefs, but I do not regret anything in my life, because I am the culmination of all of my past, both the good and the bad, and to have regret over any part of my past would be to wish I were someone else, and I can not be anyone else. I am me here, now.

Does this mean I don't think I could be a better person? Of course not. I know I can be, and that is what I strive for everyday, but I know that *because of who I am and what I've been through.* Had my life gone differently, would I have the self awareness that I do now? I don't know, just as we can never know if our lives would be better or worse. I am here, I am shaped by the totality of my life, and I can not change what has come before me. I can only grow from it.

Acceptance

Acceptance is a word we need to be sure we have a firm understanding on, not because it carries so much extra weight, but because without being at some sort of peace with where we are in our lives right now, we're never going to be able to move forward in a positive way. We have no foundation without accepting the world as it is. Acceptance is the station where we get on the change train.

Now, I know that sounds almost oxymoronic. If we accept things as they are, doesn't that mean things will never change? Not at all. We accept things as they are *in order to change them.* Think of it this way. You're the quarterback of a football team. In the huddle you call a play, but when you step to the line of scrimmage, you see that the defense is lined up perfectly to stop your play dead in its tracks. At this moment you have to accept the defense. That is what is, and now you make *your* change. You can't change the defense, just like you can't change anything outside of your control, so you have to accept it as what it is you have to deal with and you change yourself. Instead of just blindly running the play you called (in other words, instead of just doing what you've always done and not getting where you want to with it), you call an audible, you make a change (you say to yourself "I'm going to do something different") and you throw the game winning touchdown, win the Super Bowl, get mobbed by cheerleaders and tell the world you're going to Disneyland. But to do all of that, you have to accept things as they are *right now*.

Acceptance pretty much forms the basis of where we decide to take our lives, and what we are willing to do in our lives. Every day we make decisions based on that thought, that premise, so often that we don't even notice we are doing it, and we all have different levels of how much we are willing to accept. Think about going to work in the morning. That in itself is a decision based on acceptance: will I accept the parameters of this specific job? Will I accept the length of this commute? (Or perhaps more accurately, how long a commute am I willing to accept?) Will I accept it if the coffee shop doesn't have my favorite type of coffee one morning? Don't laugh. Sometimes that is a more inflexible rule than anything else. Those are only a few examples. Some, like the commute, are usually thought out in advance and accepted on a one time basis, and it has to be. If a person accepts a 30 minute drive to the office, then they have to accept it every day. It is not something they can choose to accept the first three days of the week only to not accept it the fourth, unless they call out sick. Others, like the wrong type of coffee, are a spur of the moment decision that you may not even realize is an active decision. Take it a step further. You order your coffee, pay for it, get outside, take a sip and realize it isn't what you ordered. Do you take it back and complain, or accept it and move on?

The truth is we are constantly making these bargains, striking deals with ourselves as we go through life. It is as if we are negotiating with ourselves, but instead of drawing a line in the sand over a salary demand ("I'll ask for this much, counter with that much, and accept this much.") we more often than not argue on such a fine slippery slope that we don't even realize we are losing ground.

Don't believe me? Have you ever found yourself asking "How did I wind up here?"

Acceptance of yourself

The closest I ever came in my life before now to asking the question of "why am I here?" was in self-indulgent bull-shit sessions in college, where my friends and I would ponder, and dare to answer, the larger version of that question: "Why are we here?" We thought we could save the world, even though some of us didn't even know how to save ourselves. And in the years that transpired, I never thought to come back to it on a personal level. Only lately, over the last few years, did I even begin to consider the more appropriate question for myself. Sure I could answer it. Just draw up a map of where I had been at what points in my life and sum it up with a "and that's how I got here. Any questions?"

Of course there are, because I hadn't answered the question in the first place. Simply putting push pins on a map that was hung over a timeline got me no closer to the truth than consulting a magic eight ball and getting a "Try again later" answer would. And I found out that even if you answer the question on a more emotional/personal level, if you don't find a new way of doing things, it doesn't take you away from there. The scenery may look different for a while, but you'll soon realize you're walking in the same neck of the woods, and it is because of what I accepted, and what I was willing to accept, that brought me to that point.

I don't want to confuse "acceptance" with "passive", and that is a point that needs to be very clear. People will read the word accepted and believe I am trying to say that I had no control over how my life was going. I had total control. I could have said "no" every time I said "yes" and "yes" every time I said "no". I could have chosen to stay in places I moved from and chose not to take the jobs that I took. It isn't that I was unwilling to take control of my life, but rather that I chose to accept certain things into my life.

I chose to accept fear. Fear that I would not be able to compete successfully in the market I wanted to. Fear that I did not have the ability to achieve the dreams I had laid out for myself. Fear that I would find out that I didn't have the abilities I thought I did.

I chose to accept social over professional. It became more important to me to be sure I had plenty of friends around me, that I was the life of the party and that everyone was having a good time than it was for me to focus on where I wanted to be going and living the life I believed I always wanted.

I chose to accept stability. Many people find that hard to believe when they find out how many places I've lived and how often I moved on short notice to places I knew little about. But I always moved back to the same place, the place that was comfortable, that was solid, that was the same place I dreamt about leaving for the first 18 years I was alive.

And in return for all of that, I chose to accept less than who I was. I chose to accept a facsimile of myself; I chose to accept the failure in myself. I chose to accept that which I thought I never would want in return for no longer feeling the fear of becoming who I knew I was. And finally I chose to accept a way to escape inside of all of that, a way to make me believe that the life I was living was the fantasy, and that the escape was reality.

These were the bargains that I had made with myself over the years, and before I could start becoming the person I wanted to be, the person who I knew myself to be, I had to accept these things. These were not easy things to say to myself. In the bluntest of terms, I had to look at myself and say, "I am a failure, and I accept that as where I am in my life." Later you'll read the story of the first time I did that and just as a preview let me tell you now that it did not go well at all. I couldn't accept it at first. I had to live with the truth of it for a while before I could really look at it, at what my life had become, and say, "Enough. From here I move forward." And even in doing that I had to accept that I had been living in fear, that I had willingly followed through poorly on the decisions I had made, and that I was not the person I thought myself to be. Heavy, painful stuff. Think of it as emotional growing pains.

In accepting things about oneself, there comes with that a very close relationship with limitations, and it is a schizophrenic relationship at that. Right now, in our lives at this moment, we have limitations, but that doesn't mean we have to keep them. In fact, if you are still reading this, I think it's a safe assumption that there are some limitations that you don't want anymore. That's really how we make changes in our lives and improve upon the people we are: we find our limitations and we work through them. But before we do that, we need to do one thing.

We need to accept who we are, right now.

This is true for all parts of who we are. You accept your limitations and, more importantly, your abilities. It is the unspoken hope that we then improve our abilities in order to eliminate our limitations. Everything we do is based on this awareness. If you are a good bowler, for instance, and you accept your abilities at it, it would make sense for that to be the hobby you pursue. You choose your jobs because you accept the abilities you have that fit the requirements. Once you start doing the job, or taking up that hobby, you will most likely discover that you do have some limitations that you were unaware of, but accepting those limitations gives you the place to start from in cultivating new abilities.

Let's go back to the bowling example. If you have never bowled in your life you are not going to wake up one morning and say to yourself "Self, I think we should go out and join the Professional Bowler's Tour today." You haven't accepted anything about it. You don't know how well you bowl; you probably don't even know if you like to bowl. That's not to say that you can't make an active decision in your life to someday be a professional bowler and then start working towards that goal. What it does say, what is at the core of this point is that *Right Now You Are Who You Are*. You need to know who that is and accept it so that you have a foundation to build from.

Sometimes that means accepting things you don't like. Sometimes you have to accept some ugly truths about yourself-habits that you have taken on, patterns of behavior that have become part of your personality-but these are probably the more important things to accept. It doesn't do you a lick of good to accept that you are a fantastic hard working employee if you also don't accept the fact that you, say, cheat on your spouse. While there is always certainly room to improve on the positives in our lives, it is the negatives that hound us and require our attention and our nurturing.

The important thing to remember in this is a phrase I used earlier and will go back to again over and over. That phrase is *Right Now*. Accepting who you are right now does not mean you have to continue to accept this person for the rest of your life. A while ago I accepted that I was the heaviest I'd ever been and that I didn't want to be that heavy anymore. If I didn't accept that, if I chose to not acknowledge that truth, then I would not do anything about it. So I accepted who I was, I accepted the limitations I had on it, which for me included a sedentary lifestyle, not a very good diet and no real eating plan, and I also accepted my abilities, such as being physically able to work, financially able to join a gym as well as tapping into a support network of friends for support and encouragement. Today, when it comes to addressing the issue of my weight, I no longer accept what I had to before. I no longer have the limitation of an improper diet. I have the added ability of better physical stamina so that I can increase my workout load and further my weight loss. However I also accept that I still have work to do and a ways to go before I reach my goal.

You have to be able to accept yourself, warts and all, before any change can happen. This is one of those times where it is truly about the self. It is not what others say about you or think about you or who they accept you as. It is who you accept yourself as and, just as importantly, what you plan on doing about it. It does you no good to say "I accept myself for who I am and don't need to change a damn thing."

There is always room for improvement.

There is always another step we can be taking.

But we can't take any of those steps before we know just exactly who it is that is stepping off.

Acceptance of others

Nobody wants to change. Nobody says to themselves, "Hey you know what will be fun? Confronting and addressing my shortcomings!" We only end up here because the thought of not doing something about what is going on in our lives seems more painful and burdensome than doing something about it, but only slightly. Think about it. Whatever brought you to this point did not happen all at once. You may think it did, but that was only the final action that caused you to have to confront it. I was shopping for pants, grabbed a bunch with the waist size I normally get, went into the fitting room, and realized I had gotten too big for those. I didn't suddenly get fat overnight. It was something that I hade been (not) dealing with for years, but no matter how much I bitched about it or said, "Gee, I should really do something about it" I didn't until it got to a point that I had to face. Likewise with anything else in our lives that we have some modicum of control over, it does not happen all at once, and only when the scales (the metaphoric ones, not necessarily just the physical ones) finally tip do we realize that we need to do something about it. And so we do, usually kicking and screaming and fighting it every inch of the way as we start.

In these first steps, more than doubt what we usually feel is an angered dissatisfaction, a "why me" sort of put upon feeling. Even if we have manifested no outside evidence of this change, even if the only change we made is acceptance that we have to change, that we *want* to change, we know this to be true and we look out at the rest of the world and we say to ourselves "Why us? Why not them? What makes these people better that they don't have to change and I do?"

The answer is absolutely nothing. The truth is all people have room for improvement. Everyday we all have the opportunity to live a better life than we have been living. I believe it is our responsibility to always take advantage of that opportunity, even though you may think very few people do. When you look around at everyone else, it may seem that a lot of people aren't doing a thing about it, but instead just plowing through life, some blissfully, some agonizingly. That's just part of your perception.

You see, if you were to somehow be able to stop time and go up to each and every one of those people that you think is "better" than you and find out who they really are and what their struggles in this world are, I think you would be very surprised. You would find out that fewer people are as happy as you see them to be. You would find that I did not choose the phrase "struggles in this world" just because it sounded good, but because everyone has issues in their lives. And most surprisingly to you would be when you discovered that some of these people are actively working on their struggles. They have looked at themselves and said, "I accept who I am here and now, but starting here and now, I choose to be. . ." whatever. A better spouse, more successful in or begin a new career, lose weight, quit smoking, have more patience, drink less, dance more, whatever it was that they always knew they should be but somehow got away from. In other words, you'd see something you never expected.

Everyone is just like you and me.

But it is hard to see that at first, and we become a petulant child, stomping our feet and saying why can't we have what they have. Even when we don't know what it is that they have or don't have. We just look at them and think they're better than us and we don't like it.

Funny thing happens down the line. Time goes by and whatever it is we worked on, whatever issue in our live we were questioning, becomes improved upon. (I won't say complete. I won't ever say complete. More on that later.) And now we no longer look at everyone else and think "They are all better than me." We look at them and think "I am better than all of them." I'm not saying we should, but I am saying it happens. An ex-smoker looks at someone lighting up and says "I quit smoking. I'm better than that person." A man looks at a couple fighting and says "I'm a more caring husband. I'm better than that person." Whatever the case may be, the moment will come when we are full of pride over what we have accomplished, and instead of using the good energy that the pride generates in us as a way to help ourselves keep growing forward, we instead lord it over other people, to let them know how good we've become.

Let's get that time stoppage machine again, shall we? Let's find out what's going on in their lives. Are you better than some of them? Maybe, but not nearly as many as you think you are. A better question to ask is if measuring yourself against others is even the best way to go about finding out how you are you doing.

There's a great old poem (but not nearly as old as most people think) called the Desiderata. I keep a copy of it over my desk, read it to myself three or four times a day. (Probably don't need the copy anymore, I'm sure I've got it memorized, but it's nice to look at.) A basic description of it is that it's a poem to help you live a better life. One line in particular fits perfectly with what I'm talking about:

"If you compare yourself with others you may become vain and bitter, for always there will be greater and lesser persons than yourself."

This is a very important thought, probably one of the most important ones to consider at a time like this in your life. Once you accept yourself for who you are and what it is you are trying to improve in your life, it is just as important that you accept others for whom they are on their own, and not who you think they are. If you find yourself comparing yourself to other people, you'll end up making excuses as to why they could do what you can't. Everything from the objectively tangible, "They had more schooling." "They're from a better off family." "They're younger." "They are in better shape." to the less definable, "They have more will power." "They have less stress at home." "They are naturally better at it than I am." It will take you forever if you think of yourself as inferior to other people who have gone before you. Every brain surgeon had a first day of med school. Every golfer had a first morning at a driving range. Every spouse had a first moment of doubt and insecurity. You are not born lesser than anyone, and there is nothing that says some people can grow more than others.

And this is important both when first starting out as it is when you start to feel and see and live the results. When we first decide that the time is right, and we look at ourselves and find ourselves lacking, we can not transpose our feelings onto anyone else. If we are trying to quit smoking and we have a friend who smokes more than we do, it is not our place to say "He should quit too". He is his own person. We have to accept him for who he is. We decide to improve our self esteem, and every morning when we stop to get our coffee and there is that one guy who looks like he always has his shit so together that it makes us angry, it is not our place to judge him, to wonder what secret he's hiding. Nor is it our place to be envious of him. We accept him for who he is, just as we have to accept everyone, because it is not them we are worried about and focused on. It is us.

Yes there are some technical exceptions. If you realize that what you need to do is stop smoking crack, and there are people in your life that smoke crack, you may not want to accept them as people you want to keep in your life. *But to do that, you have to first accept them as people who smoke crack.* You have to accept people for who they are. You then have the right to choose whether to accept them as part of your life.

On January 1st, 2009, after twenty five years, I quit smoking.

Yes, I am very proud of it, but do I lecture other people, tell them they should stop? Do I tell them how much better I feel, how much better my clothes smell, how much more energy I have, how I'm in better shape than they are now? Nope, partially because in some cases that last one isn't even true. Hell, I let them smoke in my car if they want to. I accept my friends who smoke. That's part of who they are. I'm no better than they are because I quit, and I don't look down on them when they step out to have a cigarette. To be sure, I have been asked by several people for advice on how I did it, and I help and support them all I can, but I don't get offended if they start again, because it is not about me versus anyone else. I have to accept others because they are on their journey just as I am on mine, and to be successful on mine, I have to know that they can accept me just as readily.

(One note, though, back to the crack smoking example. If a friend of mine were to be a crack smoker, I would probably say something. Not because I think I'm better than they are, but because I wouldn't want them to die.)

Acceptance by others

Once upon a time I was in Milwaukee for business. We were scheduled to be there for about two months and one of the perks lined up for us was free membership in the gym across the street from the hotel where we were staying. Hearing that, I said something to the effect of "it would be nice to work out again" or "time to get back into shape." Something along those lines. I can't remember exactly what I said, but I damn well remember what one of my coworker's said:

"You're a beer drinking carny whose hobby is playing poker. What kind of shape do you think you need to be in?"

To take nothing away from this person, that is exactly what I was at the time. And it was certainly something that I was happy with being. It's not as if I had gone out dressed in the emperor's finest new clothes and he was the first to see them for what they were. The reason I start with that little anecdote is because I think it is a fine way to get to the third part of acceptance, acceptance by others.

One of the toughest things you are going to have to do (and you are going to have to do it at some point) is face other people with what it is you are working on. I know I said in the beginning that this process is something that requires help from all places, but there is a time and a place to ask for that help. Two innate traits of human beings are that we are curious and we are (unfortunately) judgmental. People will want to know what you are doing, and once they know, they will tell you what they think about it. Although what they tell you will undoubtedly cover a wide spectrum, they can basically be broken down into two groups. One group of people will judge you in a good way, congratulating you on making the effort and wishing you well. The second group will laugh, call you crazy, and tell you all the other things you should be worried about. (These are the same people, by the way, who ask people that are expecting what they plan on naming the child, then proceed to tell them why those are bad choices.) With both of these groups it is a perfect opportunity to work on accepting others. Even the most well-meaning person from that first group may inadvertently say the wrong thing. They may think they are being helpful when they say stuff like "You don't need to change." or "Everything is fine. Don't worry about it." Positive affirmations are great and essential when we use them *in conjunction* with self focus, but independently they are just words. Likewise they might say the wrong thing at a time when we are fragile, starting a new and uncertain phase of growth. These words might cause more damage than good, leading us to think that we shouldn't be making these changes, and making us want to give up.

Think about it. You've gotten to this point because you have been persuaded by repetitive words and actions that have created habits in you that guide your actions, habits you now want to break. But if, in telling someone what it is you're doing, and their response, "You don't need to do that, you're fine the way you are", that is only going to positively reinforce the bad habits you're trying to break. They are trying to do what they think is the right thing by being positive and supportive to you, but instead of reinforcing the new choice and the forward action, they are instead dismissing your new focus and helping to diminish your desire for change. In fact, there is probably less positivity in a friend saying, "You don't need to change" than there is in a friend saying "About time you did something about it." (Granted, that second example only goes as far as the intention behind it. If they proceed to point and laugh at their "crazy friend" you may want to avoid that person for a while.)

Oftentimes people from the second group will say what they say from a place of ignorance or fear. Either they are not aware that there is a better way that a person can be living, or they are and they are afraid to go there. Here you come with your awareness and your courage, daring to be different, and it is not something they are willing or able to confront. Many more than that come from a defensive place of misinterpreting what you are saying as a judgment of them. I was talking with a friend once, wrestling with the identity of who I was, where I was living and how I didn't feel it was enough for me when he snapped at me quite unexpectedly. Here was a good friend of mine that I had known for years, who we had each been there for the other during tough times in our lives, getting mad at me because I was questioning my life. What finally came out of it was that, not having the life I had, not having the same dreams, same desires, but seemingly living very similar lives at the time, he took my questioning of my life as me insulting him. Basically he thought I was implying that his life wasn't good enough for me. I had to make him understand that I wasn't comparing our lives to each other, and it wasn't a matter if something was better than the other, but rather that his life is not my life, and vice versa. To help make my point I asked him "Would you want to live the life I had and do the things I want to do?" He emphatically and immediately said no, and that helped him understand that just because I was looking to make some changes in my life it didn't mean I thought everyone had to. It served to help strengthen our friendship and now, even though he doesn't always understand what I do (usually, he just shakes his head and laughs) he supports me in my endeavors. He is still my friend and still looks out for me, and will engage me in questions if he is concerned about a decision I may be making, and his counsel has proved worthwhile many times over.

One common trait both of these groups share is the seemingly instinctual need people have to say *something*, even if we're not sure what that something is. A tragic example is of course seeing someone who has just lost a loved one. A much more comedic example, one I've been on both sides of, is going backstage to see a friend who just performed horribly in a play. We feel the need to speak in situations where we are unsure what to say, partially because we want to offer support or solace or guidance or comfort, and partially because we believe the person wants to hear something from us. We assume they are waiting, much like we feel we would be, for words of agreement or validation to be offered to them.

The tough thing with getting acceptance from others about what you're are going through is that if they don't have a shared experience then they can't relate to it, and it makes it harder for them to understand what you're up against. Change does require support, though, and ultimately it will require the support of those that are around you. But initially, when the steps you are taking on this journey are new and uncertain, the support you should look to is that of other people who are in your situation or have gone through it. There's this great invention out there, maybe you've heard of it. It's called the internet, and I guarantee you there is a support group for whatever it is about you that you are looking to change. Lose weight? Check. Quit smoking? Yup. Switching careers? You betcha. Thirty seconds in a search engine and you will have resources at your fingertips you never thought possible. Support, advice, information and most importantly compassion from people who have been where you are and know what you're going through.

Now the story I told about my friend who got upset with me has, ultimately, a positive outcome. It was an outcome that was fought for, and it was in many ways very similar to many other chapters of my life that he had seen. For me to be on this journey is not something new to most people who know me. What makes it different now is that this journey has become more purposeful and guided. I am no longer simply going where the wind seems to blow me, but rather I am setting the course and plotting my way. But like all journeys, very few people want to see you leave the harbor. That's why it is important not only who you confide things in, but how you do it.

Expectation and Obligation

It is almost impossible to imagine living without a certain level of expectations. Some of the simplest things that we don't even think about we make a decision based on expectation. It's Friday night and you want to go to the movies. What are you going to see? Something that you *expect* to enjoy. Unless you're a masochist, then you might pick something you *expect* to hate. Either way, there is an expectation at play here. After the movie when people ask you how it was, you'll probably end up saying things like "Loved it. It was everything I expected it to be." Or "Hated it. Not at all like I expected." Even during the movie the phrase "Didn't expect that to happen" might pop out of your mouth. You can see just how important expectations are to us.

To achieve a fanatical inner peace one of the things you would probably want to do would be to remove all expectations from your life. A lofty and noble goal to be sure, and if that is something you eventually achieve that will truly be wonderful, but let's start with some baby steps here, okay? You can't do anything about other people and expectations they may place on you, and it's not the easiest (nor most practical) to stop having expectations of things outside of your control, like the movie, so when we talk about expectations and the need to stop having them, we are talking about the ones you place on yourself.

Recognizing these expectations, like everything else, takes time, practice, patience and forgiveness. Time to make it an organic part of who you are, practice in being able to let go of expectations, patience in understanding that it is not something that happens overnight, and forgiveness for when you get angry at yourself for not progressing as fast as you would like to. (In other words, you can't have expectations about letting go of your expectations.) But the first step in letting go of them is understanding why they are a roadblock and how to recognize them when they sneak up on you.

An expectation is nothing more than an unsubstantiated opinion of what you believe is going to happen, and they become most treacherous when you begin to have them about how it is you should be living. The expectations that you put on yourself are the ones you will never live up to. By having an expectation of what it is you are going to do, it keeps it always in your consciousness, and

30

everything you do is measured against if you are living up to it. You end up constantly focused on this mental scoreboard and it keeps you from living in the moment and experiencing what is really happening. I didn't expect to quit smoking, and I didn't have an expectation of what it would be like. Sure I had heard plenty of stories about how tough it was, and most people who found out that I had quit were not shy about telling me what a challenge I was in for, but I knew that *I was the one quitting at this moment in my life, and that had never happened before*, so how could I have any expectations as to what it would be like? Without the expectation that most people think you should have—"This is going to be really hard. I hope I can do this. What do I do when I get my cravings?"—I removed any of that outside pressure. It was just me and my desire to quit.

It is just as important to have acceptance of ourselves as it is to reject expectations of what is going to happen. Acceptance is present. It concerns the here and the now and is the base from where we grow. Expectation is future, and since none of us have created time travel yet, there is no way to know what the future holds, so stop trying to predict it and then living up to it. In reading this book, you probably have expectations about how this book is going to help you. You expect this book to make you, in some way, a better person. But if you are constantly holding on to that expectation, you will always be living in the future and not in the present where you can actually be doing the work that will make you a better person.

In the end it's a fine line, and basically a matter of semantics between the words "want" and "expect". You want to improve your life, that's why you're here, and in wanting to do something you give yourself the energy to go forward, do the work and make the improvements that you are looking for. In expecting to improve your life, you have already put yourself mentally at the finish line, one that doesn't actually exist. Expectation creates a finality that does not exist in life. Going back to the movie again, you can expect a happy ending in it, because the movie eventually ends. The credits roll, the lights come up and you go home. In the real world, life keeps happening. There is no moment where it all comes to an end. (Well, there is *one* moment, but at that point, I don't think you'll be worried about expectations.) Yes it is important that you stop and check in with yourself every so often, but that is to see where you are at, and not where you expect to be in the future.

Obligations are a lot like expectations in the sense that they are all but impossible to get away from. You have an obligation to go to work, to spend the holidays with your in-laws, to not punch the person in line in front of you who is taking waaaaaaaaay more time than any one person should ordering their food at McDonald's (even though you may feel like you'd be doing the world a favor.) And so, like expectation, we need to remove that word from your vocabulary when dealing with the one thing you can control: yourself.

Obligation is just another word that has taken on more weight than it deserves, and it is now hard to think of the word without also feeling the negative connotations that come with it. There are two kinds of obligations that we have to deal with, active ones, where we have a commitment to someone or something already stated that we need to fulfill, and passive ones, where we feel a need to fulfill a promise that has not been made. A simple example of the difference is a phone call. You told your spouse you would call them when you got to wherever you were headed (active) versus a friend calls and leaves a message, doesn't say anything about you needing to call back, but you feel like you should anyway (passive). Both of them are so much easier and less stressful to deal with when you stop thinking about them as obligations. We'll start with the active one first.

You've driven six hours to get to wherever it is you need to be. Maybe it's been a hellacious drive, loaded with traffic, construction and bad weather. You're stressed out and all you want to do when you get out of the car is relax. Or maybe the minute you get there your best friend puts a drink in your hand and tells you some wonderful news and you just want to celebrate. Or your boss meets you and takes you to dinner with the very important client you've been brought in to impress. In the middle of whatever it is you think "Oh man, I have to call my spouse." (And if you have to do something, it's just another way of saying you are obliged to do something.) You think about it in terms like that, as an additional layer to everything else that is going on, and it creates stress and confusion and worry about what is important and what you are doing next, but if you look at it a different way, it's the simplest thing to deal with.

When you over think something, that is when it takes on a

life of its own inside our heads. You don't think of every little thing you do when you check into a hotel. You don't stop at the door to your room and say "Okay, first I'm going to turn on the light, then put down my bag, then go to the bathroom, then take off my shoes, then turn on the televisions, then, then, etc., etc., etc." (At least I hope you don't.) You simply just do all that stuff. The phone call is no different. You simply make it. You're not obliged to do it, just like you know you're not obliged to take off your shoes. You just know it's something you're going to do.

It's the same with the passive obligation. Your friend calls, leaves a message, says "goodbye", and you sit there and think, "Oh man, I have to call him back." And you start thinking about it. Should you call him back now? Should you wait until later? Did they sound like it was important? Do you have time to talk right now? Here's an easier question to ask yourself:

Do you want to talk to them right now? If yes, dial their number, if not, don't. It's as simple as that. And even if they said in the message "Hey call me back" you can still ask yourself the same question, because you are under no obligation (there's that word again) to drop what you're doing and call them.

Now both of these examples have an element I didn't take into account and that is the element of emotional connectedness, but in both cases it would only serve to further separate your action from considering it an obligation. If you had a hellacious drive, or good news to share, or an important event was about to happen, I would think you would want to call your spouse (you know, the whole other half of the love you until death do you part thing) for comfort, for elation or for support. Likewise if a friend leaves a message, someone you care about, you are probably more genuinely interested in calling them back, whether they asked you to or not, than you would some stranger trying to sell you vinyl siding.

Obligation is nothing more than unnecessary weight put on something we already want to do, or at least accept that we have to. We may not want to go to work, but we know that we have to, so it is best just to accept that and move on, and not gnash our teeth and shake our fist at the sky, cursing our employment. If you remove that emotional/mental weight from it, you will find it might actually be more enjoyable than you thought. It's no different then when a person loses physical weight, how much better they feel, not just physically, but emotionally as well. To begin making it part of who you are, start with the simplest things, the things in your own personal life. You're not obliged to tell your spouse you love them; you tell them because you feel it. You're not obliged to rake the leaves; you do it because the sense of pride it gives you to see how well you take care of your space. You're not obliged to move on to the next part of this book, the part where I tell you just how I came to start this journey; you do it because you want to.

Enough about you. Let's talk about me.

There was the way that I had become. Now there was the way I was going to be. To tell this story, there are a couple of things you have to recognize.

Rock Bottom

There is a phrase I'm sure all of you are familiar with: Rock bottom. When you finish reading this story, I will not be surprised if many of you say "That's what he considers rock bottom? That's not even close. Why I know stories of people who" and fill in your own blank of what they have gone through to come out the other side. Whole families dying in tragedy, horribly unspeakable acts done to satisfy addictions, harrowing ordeals involving natural disasters or accidents, all of these surely make mine pale by comparison. The fact of the matter is that events like that don't happen nearly as often as the specials on FOX would have you believe. Sure, I guarantee that you can't go a week watching your local news without seeing a story that fits the above description. They're heartwarming tales that boost ratings and, more importantly, give us all hope that there is a positive result to the challenges that life throws at us. But for every one event like that, I'm sure there are a thousand stories of people making a stand in their life and changing it for the better that you've never heard of. Why? Because there wasn't a film crew there when the twelve year old boy who got tired of being in the drug game told himself "I'm not going to be like this anymore" and went back to school, got a part time job to support himself and became successful at who he wanted to be. There wasn't a reporter handy the day the single mom got fed up with waiting for the child support payments that were always late stood up and said "I'm not going to live like this anymore." And no one bothered to call the newspaper the day you looked at your life and said "I can be better." It happens all the

35

time, and just like it takes a long time for us to come out of these dark places, it takes a long time for us to get in them. If I were to sit down and look back over my life, I'm sure I could find several (dozen) examples of choices I made that led me to where I ended up, and I'm sure that at the time, if someone asked me, I would have defended them. It is not a singular moment that occurs. The twelve year old boy saw drugs around him his whole life. The single mom dealt with months, if not years, of neglect. You have recognized many times where you wanted to grow. The moments simply add up until they reach a critical mass. It becomes a matter of what one is willing to take before they finally stand up and say I'm mad as hell and I'm not going to take it anymore! We all have a different level of that. If my level were higher, I might have become a successful actor by this point, because I wouldn't have accepted anything to get in the way of my dreams. If it were lower, I'd probably be passed out in a drunken stupor on the beach right now. Look at everyday life. We all make concessions along the way, whether it be the people we allow ourselves to associate with, the environment we are going to raise our children in, the destructive behaviors we are going to indulge ourselves in. These are continual choices that we constantly reaffirm until one day we just say no. We just stand up and say no.

The second thing to be on the lookout for is the confirmation of what I said at the beginning of this book: *We do nothing on our own.* And here's where our story begins.

Moving to Key West

Moving down to Key West to find one's self is much like moving to Ethiopia to study the mating habits of penguins. It can probably be done, but there are a lot of strikes against you from the get go. Most people move to Key West to lose themselves, and more than a few of them succeed. I'm not just talking about the resident crazies who seem to have nothing better to do than ride their bikes all day (although there are days when I figure that ain't such a bad way to be.) I mean people who on the surface look very much like all their oars reach the water. Once you get to know them, however, it's a whole new ballgame. I worked with one guy who was convinced that Osama Bin Laden was out to get him, and that the C.I.A. had snipers on the rooftops of all the buildings that surrounded our restaurant, ready to take him out. I'm not making this up. The best was when I walked through the kitchen and found him yelling "I can't listen to you and write this down at the same time." Not so odd, until you learn that there wasn't anyone talking to him. At least not outside his head. Inside was probably a whole other story. And this guy held a job, which just goes to show you the relative level of crazy that inhabits the island. But that was my reason for coming here. I needed to go someplace, and I couldn't think of anywhere better to go, especially when I woke up that morning in Delaware and it was nine degrees with three inches of snow on the ground. Within an hour I was e-mailing friends, and within a month I had arrived.

There were personal goals I wanted to achieve in moving to Key West. Lose some weight, write more regularly, get into (somewhat) better shape, and work on getting vices under a bit of control. The first three were easy enough to do, more or less. It was that last one that was a bitch.

Looking back, of course, there were serious flaws in my choice. The decision was made somewhat rashly, based mostly on the weather. One other important factor was that, while I knew some people, I didn't know them well, and I didn't know many. My friends, and I will forever be thankful to them, helped me get set up, but for the first time in twelve years of moving around, I was not falling into a prearranged social scene where I knew all the players and activities. I needed a fresh start where I could establish a new way of living.

Unfortunately, humans are social creatures. We gravitate towards other humans. Not necessarily a bad thing, but in Key West it is magnified a thousand times by the sheer nature of the location. Every time I think about my decision I am reminded of the movie "St. Elmo's Fire". More precisely, I am reminded of a brilliant spoof of it that I saw in Los Angeles performed by a very talented sketch comedy group called the Film Pigs. As they re-enact one of the final scenes, where the Rob Lowe character is getting on the bus bound for New York, one of the actors had a line that was something to the effect of "I'm glad he's going to New York. There he'll have no problem getting over his drinking problem." You think it's tough to kick the bottle in the Big Apple? Try it on Bone Island.

In New York City, if you want to drink, there are a million ways to do it. But if you don't want to drink, then there are a million other things to do to distract you. Name it, and they probably have an amateur society of it somewhere in New York. And not just what one would traditionally think of as city things. Oh, no. They have whitewater rafting clubs, downhill skiing clubs, golf clubs, even bird watching clubs. You name it, they got it. What they also have are about, on average, something like a couple dozen A.A. meetings a day, if not more. (I looked it up once, you know, just for kicks.) And if A.A. ain't your cup of tea, there are other organizations out there to help you stop drinking. So, not only does New York give you countless avenues to stop drinking, they also give you a hundred times as many options of things to do to distract you from the fact that you're not drinking. Key West? Not so much.

Thing is, I didn't want a distraction from it. I hadn't wanted a distraction from it for the last fifteen years, why should I want one now? My life had been, for better or worse, one long roaming cocktail party from the time I was barely nineteen and living in New York City in the fall of 1990, making stops in San Francisco, Los Angeles, New York a couple of times, and a few layovers back in Connecticut, not to mention any number of 2,3,4 and more day vacations I could sneak in there, whether it was a day at a Jimmy Buffett concert (a vacation if only in the mind) or a week in The Bahamas, before finally depositing me in Key West in January of 2005. It was as if my whole adult life had been a long training period for *just this moment.* And for just over a year I embraced it. But then it wasn't enough.

Think about it. I wake up one morning in a beautiful house I share with two really good friends of mine. I live in a tropical paradise tending bar and making a very good living. You know how people aspire to have the job with the corner office? My corner office was a Tiki bar that overlooked the sunset. Top that. I was well liked by lots of people, respected by those who employed me and was having a great time every day and night. What more could I have asked for? Apparently a lot, because in the middle of all of this I said to myself, "This is not who you are, and this is not where you are supposed to be." Funny thing happened at that point.

Nothing.

"Come to Jesus"

There are lots of names and phrases for that moment when everything changes in a person's life. In AA, they call it a "moment of clarity". Other people say that they have finally "seen the light". The phrase my roommate used, however, was the one that stuck with me. He called it a "Come to Jesus" moment. Now, my friend is not a religious person and, in spite of having two immediate family members in the ministry, I'm not exactly a poster child for piety (Bartender in Key West, remember?) and it isn't meant in a religious way. It simply was a way to describe the opening of one's eyes to finally see the forest for the trees if you will. (I will mix metaphors with the best of them.) This was my moment, my come to Jesus, when I saw the world not for how I imagined it to be, but for what it was. Did I have a good life, maybe, but all the dreams I had fostered for so many years were as far from me as anything could be. Everything I had set out to be, everything I prided myself on being, had fallen to the wayside as I skirted around the country chasing one good time after the next. That time was over. It was time for me to start living the life I was destined to, time to start living my life period, and not let life live me. To paraphrase W.H. Auden, I owed it to the world to get on with what I was good at. So I did.

I drank myself deeper. I crawled into the bottom of the bottle (one of my friends wryly mentioned that it wasn't too far a crawl) and I stayed there for three months, embarrassed by how I had let go of all of my dreams and ashamed to talk to anyone who knew me. I kept up a good façade for the people I knew on the island, because they didn't know that I was not who I appeared to be. They didn't know me from my past, they never heard me speak of all the dreams that I let go, one by one, until they were no longer part of who I was. I could fool them, but I couldn't fool the people who had known me forever. The phone became my worst enemy. Afraid to talk to anyone I cut off communication with the whole outside world. Even my roommates in Key West could see it in me, enough so that they would carefully pick and choose when to talk to me, finding the few brief moments in the day when I was closer to sober than normal. And in those moments I knew, too, what I was doing to myself, but I couldn't think of a way to get out of it. I knew what I was doing wasn't helping the cause any, that it was only working to deepen the feelings of failure, but I was terrified, because all I could see was a hole that I had dug so deep for myself I could barely see the light at the top of it. In those brief moments I would feel the pain, and I would cry, and I would wonder aloud how I was going to fix things, but the easy answer was always to start drinking again, and that was what I did. It was the first of many paradoxes I would find myself faced with.

In all of recorded history there is the story of the immediate conversion. Faced with overwhelming odds, struggling against the tide, suddenly, miraculously everything is made clear and the person, once downtrodden, now lives immediately in grace. The stink of failure is replaced with the scent of success. Night becomes day and all is right with the world. Go watch any tear jerking movie, read any feel good novel. The change is at once, it is thorough, and it is complete. Watch "The Blues Brothers" if you want a perfect example. Literally he is bathed in the light and says "The band." Presto. All is forgiven. So, here I am, aware that my life is at its zenith, and why isn't it all changing for me just as quickly? If I recognize that my life is incomplete, doesn't it just automatically complete itself?

Apparently not. So I struggled with what to do. I thought about moving away. I thought about staying. I thought about moving in with a girl. She thought otherwise. I was latching on to anything I could that would give me some sense of stability, even if it was a false sense, just to let me know it was going to be all right. I shudder to think about who I was in those months, and it is a testimony to the strength of the human spirit and its ability to forgive and to love unconditionally that I am still friends with some of these people. But at the time I couldn't see anything but my own degeneration, as I sat at the bottom of my bottle, wondering why my Hollywood moment, my *deus ex machina* hadn't arrived yet. In the end, it turns out I just hadn't given it enough time.

My best friend, we'll call him "Patrick", had called me a number of times. The last time we had spoke I told him that I was moving home and would be in town by a certain day. Well, he called me that day, leaving a message wondering if I was in town and could I make it to a party at his house. I didn't return that call. Nor did I return the three other calls he made in as many weeks. To be fair to my friends, I have moved so often that they tend not to worry too much when they don't hear from me, but I could tell by the last message he left that he was growing a little concerned. I apparently wasn't in Connecticut, nobody else up there had heard from me, everyone was assuming I was still in Key West, but there was no confirmation of that fact. Now I was becoming even more ashamed because, not only am I a failure, I thought, I am afraid to even talk to my best friend. He has been my best friend since we were five, he was always there for me as I struggled to find my place in the world and we have shared so many great memories over the years. He has been there through my darkest days, most importantly the passing of my father. There were days I would not have been able to stand if he hadn't been there to hold me up, and I will forever be thankful that he is part of my life. So you could imagine how afraid and ashamed I must have felt if I couldn't even talk to him.

Part of me knew, though, that I couldn't not talk to him either, that I had to let him know what I was going through, so I wrote him a letter, explaining all of it, telling him how I felt lost in the world. I didn't know what I expected the outcome of the letter to be. I'm sure part of me hoped he would see it as my cry for attention, I'm sure part of me was afraid he would simply shake his head. I don't know if I even had any expectations for it. All I know is that I had to send it to him, so one Saturday morning, I put a stamp on the envelope and dropped it in the mailbox.

Eight hours later, my mother called me to tell me my uncle had passed away. This particular uncle had been a wonderful man to me and my family my whole life. If it hadn't been for him I never would have been in Key West. It was through a generous loan he made to me that I could afford to make the move in the first place. She told me the dates and times for the services, and I told her of course I would be up there for it. I hung up the phone and became very nervous. You see, every time I ventured back to Connecticut for weddings or funerals or such, I would stay with Patrick. My immediate family had all moved away as well, and staying with him gave us the opportunity to catch up for a while. I figured this time would be no different, except of course for one small problem.

The letter.

I placed a phone call the next morning, confident that it would go right to voice mail which it did. I told him the situation, asked him if it would be okay if I stayed, and then casually mentioned that maybe he should keep an eye on the mailbox before hanging up.

Three days later his cousin, also a good friend of mine, called me. Like I said, I wasn't one for answering the phone much at this time, especially if it was someone from back home, but I figured by now the letter had made it there and the cousin had been informed of it as well, so it would be better just to get this out of the way. Sure enough it had. Patrick's wife had called him and told him to call me, make sure I didn't have my head in the oven, and that of course I could stay with them. Patrick himself called me that night to confirm everything, and I remember one specific part of the conversation. I mentioned that I was renting a car to get around with so I wouldn't be a bother to anyone, and he replied.

"Yeah, you thinking you're a bother to your friends. That's something else we need to talk about this weekend."

The moment of truth

I flew up, saw all my relatives, spent time with my family, and then retreated back to Patrick's house for the weekend. Saturday night rolled around and we found ourselves sitting in his living room. At some point his wife discreetly slipped off to bed, and I knew now it was time for "The Conversation."

He asked how I was doing. I answered in generalities, not making much in the way of eye contact, not giving too much away, afraid of what might happen if I did. To give you an idea of how much pain I was in, I was convinced that this man who had known me and loved me like a brother for almost thirty years was going to pass judgment on me, and I was terrified, like a child caught and brought before his parent, who he knows will dole out the punishment. We talked for a while, and when it became clear that I wasn't going to offer much, he said the two words I guess I'd been longing to hear.

"Come home."

He told me how it would be, that I could stay for a while until I got on my feet, that with a kid on the way I couldn't stay forever, but that I needed to be there, that I needed to get away from where I was at, both physically and emotionally. He, and everyone else who knew and loved me, would do what they could to help me. I thanked him and hugged him, and told him I would do what I could to get home quickly. I had some logistics to work out, namely just exactly how I was getting home. I had no car, as it was unnecessary in Key West, but compared to what I was going through, this was hardly a problem.

What surprised me, and ironically enough saddened me a little, was that at no point in this long weekend did I have a breakdown. Not with my friends, not with my family, nothing. It was only when I was about to leave Monday morning for the airport, Patrick and his wife already gone to work for the day, did I cry. As I walked through the kitchen, there was an envelope that said "Jack Terry". I knew both from the handwriting and the way she always referred to me by both names that it was from his wife. Before I even opened it I started to well up. By the time I was done reading it, I was outright bawling.

> Jack Terry-
>
> It has been good seeing you this weekend. Patrick has shared with me that you are going through a tough time now. We have all been there my friend. When you are sorting through it all and reflecting, please remember one thing. The only attribute that matters is what's in your heart. I know it sounds fluffy but it's true, and you have one of the kindest hearts I know. I rarely hear you speak poorly of others and your capacity to love is huge! At the end of the day I think that counts for something. The rest are just limits and expectations we put on ourselves. Anyway you are in my thoughts and prayers. Keep your eyes open until you see the Jack the rest of us do!
>
> Beth

Actually, there was a little heart symbol before her name, but I didn't know how to type that.

This is a perfect example of what I meant when I said at the beginning that we do nothing on our own, and that the people who we are surrounded by are there to help define who we are and where we are going. I read this card every day. I have to. I taped it to my desk so that when I sit down to write I can see it, and it serves to remind me just how important my friends are to me and how much they care. It helps me to realize things I don't or can't always see on my own. It is an issue of knowing something versus believing something, an idea I will go into more detail about later. For now, it's back to the narrative.

As I lay in my bed that night back in Key West, I rolled over in my mind all that had happened. Sure I was excited by the possibilities, but the biggest obstacle remained in front of me, that of the car, and because of my general mindset, to me it loomed as insurmountable. None of the rest of it mattered if this couldn't be addressed.

Tuesday, the next morning, I saw the ad.

Wednesday, I went for a test drive.

Thursday, I bought it.

Friday, I registered it.

Saturday, I packed it and left.

(Sunday I blew a radiator hose and spent two days in Alexandria, Virginia.)

Tuesday, eight days after I had pulled out of Patrick's driveway in a rented, brand new Chevy Cobalt, I pulled back in driving my own, sixteen year old, Honda Accord with a quarter of a million miles on it.

Wednesday, still waiting to hear from the people I would eventually work for, I called up an old boss of mine in the restaurant business.

Thursday, I was at work.

In twelve days, it had all happened:

Questions had been asked, both by me and about me. What was I doing? Why was I doing it? What should I be doing instead? What was I going to do to change it and make it better?

Decisions had been made. Staying where I was would no longer work for me. My lifestyle I was destructive and counter productive for who I was and who I wanted to be. Furthermore, even though I have a number of friends both in New York and Los

Angeles and it would seem to make more sense to go to those locations if I wanted to once again pursue acting, I knew that I needed to heal myself first, to right my ship before I could entertain any notion of sailing it, and the best place to do it would be back where I was from and where my friends, the ones who have known me the longest and cared for and loved me so much would be there to help me walk again. My friends in New York and Los Angeles all love me too, as well, and would have made the same generous offer I'm sure, but I knew if I went to those places, it would be no different than how it was in Key West. And at the time, nothing else was even an option in my mind. When a friend of mine in Key West expressed surprise that I wanted to move to Connecticut, I asked him why he wanted to eventually move back to Phoenix. He said "Because its home. Ooohhh." He got it.

Action was taken, both for the short term and the long term. I had made the move. I had the ability get around, to find a place of my own. I had the means to begin settling in and making the changes in my life. I was working, making money, while I waited for the events concerning my eventual job, events that were primarily out of my hands, to play out. I put myself in a position of betterment.

And I certainly didn't do it alone. All along the way you can see the influence of so many other people who were there to help me. If any one of them hadn't been, there is no telling what would have happened. Without the place to stay, without the job contacts, both old and new, without the offer of moral support, all of this could have turned out so differently. It might have still happened, but I'll never know, and I don't want to find out.

Now, I may have done all these things, but it doesn't mean I was I done.

Changing clothes

When I first got home, everything felt better. Don't let that confuse you though. Just because something feels better doesn't mean it is better. Any change at all, even the littlest thing, is usually going to make you feel better. You come home from a long day at

45

work, exhausted. But the simple act of changing your clothes usually results in you feeling better. How do I know it's a matter of just feeling better, though, and not being better? You can answer that by realizing just long that feeling lasts before you realize you are still exhausted from your day.

The first several months I was back in Connecticut was one long slow change of clothing. And not just that, but it was like I was changing into the most comfortable old jeans and smoothed down t-shirt I had. Friendships picked up as if they had been left off the week before. Back at work I knew all the managers and everyone in the kitchen. The lay out of the floor was as familiar to me as the house I had grown up in. It wasn't even as if I was re-establishing my life; it was if my life hadn't happened in the time I was away, even though I had been away at that point for almost five years.

Not every choice I made at that point was the best choice I could have been making, and I know I justified some of them by playing the victim card a little bit. 'I'm going through a tough time, so I'm allowed some leeway with my decision making.' I was doing some of the same things I had been doing the last several months in Key West, partially because I could but also partially because I knew I was deluding myself into believing that just because I had "changed my clothes", my life was suddenly going to be better. But just as I mentioned before, after a while that wore off and I knew it was time to get serious.

By this point I had taken a new job, one that didn't pay well but came with amazing benefits. (There are perks to working for a non-profit.) In a short amount of time working there I became close with a co-worker and talked to her about what I had been dealing with for the better part of the past year. She recommended a therapist, I gave him a call and we set an appointment.

I had met with therapists before at various points of my life, but by this point it had been twelve years, so even though I was somewhat comfortable (after all, this was something I chose to do) I wasn't really sure what was going to happen. This was the first time I chose to meet with a therapist that I had a specific issue I felt needed to be addressed. As a kid there were behavioral issues, but I was sent to these sessions somewhat against my will. Twelve years earlier it had been right after my father died and I wanted some help dealing with my emotions over the whole thing. This time, I had a singular focus. I knew how I felt, I knew why I felt that way, and I just needed to figure out how to get through it. As such, I knew just what I expected us to talk about.

I'll pause for a moment while we silently reflect on my previous thoughts about expectations.

The first session was based, at least in the beginning, about me telling him my life story, childhood, schooling, upbringing, the whole nine. I understood it was important for him to know such things so he could get a handle on who I was, so I didn't speed through it all, but I knew (or thought that I knew) that it was all just background to the important stuff, the current stuff, and so I tried to move forward in that direction. He kept stopping me, though, and brining me back to the final years of High School and my time in college, and my dreams of pursuing acting. I remember getting frustrated after a while. I wanted to say "I don't care about of that, that's not my life anymore. I want to talk about this." Looking back I'm not sure why I didn't say any of that, perhaps knowing that being confrontational wouldn't be the best way to open up lines of communications. Besides, it was only the first session, and because of my benefits they were only costing me five dollars a visit. I figured I could give him the benefit of the doubt and go for a few weeks before I passed judgment on him and what we talked about.

Driving home that day, having time to process what we'd been talking about, I began to realize it made a lot more sense than I had thought. Having my expectations of what I thought the issue was clouded me from being able to see where the root of the problem lay. I felt like a failure because I wasn't living the life and being the person I always thought I would be, and he kept bringing me back to the point in my life where my paths diverged from who I thought I was going to be and who I ended up being. It was the first of many lights that would go off in my head over the next several months as he helped me grapple with these issues. To be sure there was plenty of other stuff we talked about, wide ranging conversations dealing with everything from mortality to fidelity, but these were all offshoots growing from the core issue that had brought me to this point in my life.

One of my toughest days was when I finally cracked through the shield I had built up around myself. Between the images I would present and the creative wording I would use to talk about why I was living the way I was and not the way I thought I was supposed to be, it was as if I created a character of myself, complete with stock answers to the oft repeated questions. In his office I couldn't use those answers because we both knew they were empty and hollow, that they were not a part of who I was. Maybe someday long ago they had been, when I first started to slip from my preconceived identity, but by now they were just words and nothing more. I remember sitting in his chair, fighting with the truth and figuring out a way to make it manifest, to the point that I couldn't sit, that the energy and the power of the emotions made me stand, made me pace, made me force myself to see it and to share, to vocalize it once and for all.

I didn't want the life I had wanted when I was that 19 year old kid who had the world by the short hairs. One good hard look at my life and any fool would have recognized that. (Well, any fool but me.) What the truth was that I wanted to live like I had been when I was that 19 year old kid. I wanted to live with the passion and the confidence and the boundless energy that crackled in me every day. The truth was that it wasn't important to me any more to be the next James Stewart or Al Pacino. The truth was that it was important to me to remember that the world was my oyster, that my options were limitless, that it didn't matter what I did but rather how I did it. It was a powerful moment, one that came after months of struggle that had followed years of neglect.

Now that I had a guidepost, we began to work on a new journey. We talked at length about finding ways to capture that power and purpose. We examined the difficulty of bringing that back to my life while being in a society vastly different from the one I had been in all those years ago. It is one thing to be a ball of nuclear fusion in the wide open spaces of an acting school in New York City. It is quite another to do that in suburban Connecticut. We looked at ways to find that balance, to determine where the balance was, and what parts of whom I was and wanted to be took priority over other parts. We set about on a mission whose goal was to repurpose me, find me a new way to live that felt both right and good to me.

And one week, it just all clicked. I didn't have to think about my choices; they happened naturally. I didn't have to obsess over what I was doing and was it the right thing; I simply knew that it was. I didn't worry about the dread that had seemed to become as much a part of me as my shadow; I could feel it fading. And so, when my next appointment rolled around, I went into the office, sat in my usual chair, and just looked at him and kind of smiled. He smiled back.

"Feels good, doesn't it?" he asked. He knew. He could tell. We talked about my week. I told him things that had happened and how I responded to them. I talked about the new found positivity that was part of me. And then I finally said, "I think I'm ready." Five minutes after I walked into his office that day, I shook his hand and walked out.

I continued to actually see him for close to another year, but much less frequently. Every six weeks or so, I would stop in for what I would jokingly refer to as a tune up. And not all of the sessions were as easy as that last one had been. Sometimes I would have set backs, end up with more on my plate than I knew how best to handle. For a little bit I did see him on a slightly more regular basis, just to help make sure I didn't slide too far back. But they all helped to remind me of the truth I had found and to keep me focused on where I was headed, even if I didn't always know where I was going. When I decided to leave Connecticut to spend time with my family, you can be sure he was one of the people I called.

I certainly don't think I'm finished. I know that I continue to grow and refine myself and my goals in this world, and to work at bringing those goals and desires into harmony with the world around me. Somewhere in the next section of the book, I talk about the elusive search for answers. When I went into his office that day with the lightness of success inside of me, I did not mistake that believing I had answers. But I did know that I had direction.

So, how we doing?

Figured we could take a little breather here, check in with ourselves and each other, stretch our legs, check the score of the ballgame, that sort of thing. And when you are ready, come back for the second half. This is the part full of pithy anecdotes and insightful observations, designed as much to amuse as they are to educate. In fact, if I'm any good, you won't even realize you learned something. Think of them as paint blazes on the sides of trees, just to help you find your way on the path.

The very first absolute truth

People are constantly trying to tell those who are younger than them that the next few years of their lives will be the best years ever. I find that kind of annoying in two different ways. First of all, nine times out of ten, they barely know who they are talking to or what they are talking about. Secondly, if the next few years are going to be the best, then what is the rest of my life going to consist of? Crap? Boy, there's a thought to make you feel good about the future.

I think people do it because they want to make someone feel good, either the talker or the talkee. Some people probably think that they are doing a favor. "Hey, kid, get ready. The next few years are going to be the greatest!" You know, kind of like a warning, so we can be ready for all the great times that are coming at us. This kind of implies an inherent stupidity on the receiver's part, of course. It is as if they are saying we would not recognize the good times that happened unless they have been pointed out to us in the first place. "What do you mean those were great times? How was I to know? Nobody told me!"

The rest of the people are trying to do themselves a favor. The years that they are talking about in our future, whether it be high school, college, our thirties or our eighties, probably were the best years for them, and they don't want to be the only ones to feel that way. They put pressure on other people to justify their own memories. If the person telling you that the next whatever set of years will be the greatest, make sure you aren't talking to some ex-homecoming king, starting quarterback for his high school who now sells insurance in the same small town he grew up in, coaches his son's little league team, has chronic heartburn and is trying to figure out how to meet the girl who works at the Dairy Queen without his wife finding out. If you are, thank him for his time, and then slowly back away, smiling the whole time so as to not alarm him. Conversely, if the guy telling you this happens to be ninety, well, he's probably some kind of expert on what years were best. Keep in mind, however, that the only years he might remember at this point are those from when he was the homecoming king, starting quarterback for his high school.

(And I don't mean anything against insurance salesmen. It's just that in a lifetime of jobs, my least favorite was my ten month stint with an insurance company. By a long shot. Best thing about it was it convinced me to move back to New York and get on with my life.)

It is true, however, that you will spend the rest of your life listening to people tell you that you are on the cusp of the best years of your life. When I was in sixth grade, I heard it about junior high. When I was in junior high, I heard it about high school. In high school, college. In college, my twenties. In my twenties, my thirties. Let me tell you something folks. I just turned forty, and if someone comes up to me and tells me my forties are going to be the greatest years of my life, he is going to get hurt.

Of course, what I dread more than that is someone coming up to me, finding out how old I am, and saying "Man, weren't the twenties the greatest years of your life?" Because then I will have to go somewhere and cry over my supposedly lost youth, and as much as I would hate to hurt someone, I hate to cry even more.

By now you are probably wondering why I think about all of this. It came from something an old boss of mine said to me a while back. To call him my boss is, while accurate, also slightly misleading. He was my boss in the sense that I got the job because of him and through him. However, he wasn't the one who set my hours or my pay, which is too bad, because if he were, I'd have gotten paid a whole lot better and worked a whole lot more consistently, but such is life. Just so you know, it was with a traveling theatrical production of a sideshow. My boss was the performer and impresario, and I was the carny trash that drove the truck, built the stage and shoveled the shit, as it were. Anyway, at some point in the process, my boss and I were back stage right before a show talking. My boss is what we like to call a giver, and we were joking about that when he said "Don't forget. I'm also a taker."

"Oh yeah? And what have you taken from me?"

"I've taken the best years of your life."

At which I laughed and responded, "If these are the best

years of my life, then I am in a world of trouble."

After the show was over, not just that performance, but that leg of the tour, I retired to my mother's house, which is where I recuperated between jobs, and thought about what he had said, what I had said, and what people had been telling me my whole life: The Best Years Of Your Life Are Right Around The Corner! (And Have Been For The Last Thirty Years!) That got me to thinking about my life; and I realized something very important. . .

The best years of my life are <u>right now</u>, and have always been.

Now I know that sounds a little "new agey" and stupid, but the fact is we don't live in the future. We don't live in the next five years, no matter what age we may be. Our next decade is not where the best things happen. The best things happen now, while we are living in the moment. There is a great quote, which I think might be from John Lennon, but could be from *Ferris Bueller's Day Off* that says "life is what happens while we're busy making plans."

Think about it.

Life is what happens while we're busy making plans.

I am always making plans and looking forward to something other than what I was doing at that moment. Whether it's having a vacation planned or going out somewhere special on my night off, I am always concerned with what is going to happen. So much so that I usually don't know what is happening right in the moment. At the end of most days I wouldn't remember much about what had happened. In my mind it had been nothing remarkable, at least not in comparison to the plans I had for Saturday night, or the vacation coming up next month, or what have you. But think about this: How many times have you made big plans with high expectations, only to find yourself even slightly disappointed with how things turned out? Hell, how many times have you made plans that have fallen through all together? You don't pay attention to anything going on during your week because there's some big party happening Friday night at your friend's house and that's all you can think about. Then, when Friday rolls around, your friend is sick, or you're sick, or you get stuck at work, or the weather turns bad, or any one of a hundred things you can't control gets in the way, and you never make it to the party. It's happened to you, it's happened to me, it's happened to everybody. So much energy wasted, so much emphasis placed on a particular future event that the here and now came and wentunnoticed. And that's why I say not even just the best years, but the best weeks, days, hours of our lives are *right now!*

(And yes, I understand that there is a difference between looking forward to your daughter's wedding this Saturday and looking forward to cleaning the garage this Saturday. Having the second may give you more opportunity to focus on the present, and the first may prove to be a bit more distracting. I'm not saying all plans are created equal. I'm just saying that regardless of what the plans are, between now and then, there is still a whole lot of present to live in.)

Just as we don't live in the future, we also don't live in the past. I've told you how the past shapes us, defines who we are to a certain degree, and certainly makes it more challenging when it comes to issues of personal identity, i.e. who we are versus who we believe we are meant to be. But it is just that: the past. What is done is done, and it can not be changed. Best we can do is learn from it, so that the next time we do better, smarter, than we did the first time. We are no longer living the high school prom, the first day of junior high, the last time we dumped someone or someone dumped us. We are living today.

Who knows the answer?

I wanted to know everything when I was a kid. I loved to ask questions. Some days I'm sure my parents wished they had hot burning spikes to stick in their ears just to give themselves a respite from my incessant questioning. Even back then I embraced the belief that an unexamined life is not a life worth living. I used to read the encyclopedia just for fun. Seriously. We had two different sets and I read them both, from cover to cover. (Can't imagine why I didn't have many friends as a kid.) And as far as Trivial Pursuit goes, you do not want to play me. Trust me on this one. I may have a hard time remembering people's birthdays, but I can tell you that Yorba Linda is where Richard Nixon's presidential library is, that Lucille Ball wore a size eight dress on "I Love Lucy", and that Hedda Hopper was the most famous gossip columnist in the 40's and 50's. Why I know these things I couldn't tell you other than it is just me wanting to know everything.

This translated into the big questions as well. I wanted to know why we were here? What was my purpose in life going to be? What did it all mean? Was there a God? And if there was did they create all this with a plan in mind or was this just a cosmic crap shoot? People tried to explain it to me in all sorts of ways, telling me that the answers would come in time, that there were no answers, and that it was just life. I also got the "why did it matter what the answers were?" response. None of that was good enough for me, so I kept searching. As I got older, I thought I found them. Those big questions, about life and existence and God? Please! My friends and I regularly dismissed such questions with the pomposity and bull-headedness that only nineteen year old undergraduates in New York City can. We would sit around coffee shops, drinking pots of coffee and eating plates of French fries, telling anyone who would listen how we knew everything. At least, I know I did. I was confident that I could tell anyone everything about anything. I knew it all. It was this conceit that got me in a lot of trouble.

When you think you know everything you stop learning. I

lived my life for years and years not bothering to learn anything new because I didn't think I needed to. The smartest I ever felt was the day I woke up and realized that I didn't know anything. Not a damn thing. And let me tell you, it took a long time, and no small amount of pride to get out of the way, before I realized that. It was at once both the most humbling and freeing moment of my life. *Humbling* because I knew that I had fallen to a whole new level. Imagine if everything you knew to be true suddenly wasn't anymore. My way of thinking, my way of being, all had been proven wrong. If I wanted to get back to the Promised Land, it was time to start working, and that was what was so *freeing* about it. I no longer was stuck to my old ways of thinking. The questions that I thought I knew all the answers to didn't even exist anymore. There were no more questions to answer, period. My preconceived notions, my misconceptions of what had been my life had all gone away and gave me the chance to start again.

In the classic science fiction novel "The Hitch Hiker's Guide to the Galaxy" bug Douglas Adams addresses this very issue. What becomes clear is that there is an answer to the universe: one answer that neatly ties everything together. The answer is *Forty-Two*. The trick is to figure out how to phrase the question. I told you earlier that this isn't a self help book. It isn't. Self help books claim to have all the answers. They will swear to you up one side and down the other that they have all the knowledge you are ever going to need. First of all, there is no such thing as *all* the knowledge you are ever going to need. Every day in life there is a chance to grow, to become more than you were the day before. The only way to do that is to learn everyday. Secondly, and I don't care who they are, no one can give you the answers, because the answers they have are not the answers you need. Think about it: Is anyone just like you? No. There are people that are similar. Maybe they have the same career as you; maybe they have the same cancer as you. Maybe they live in the same neighborhood you do, maybe they went to the same college. Maybe, just maybe, they are so like you it's scary. Maybe their house looks the same, they drive the same car, root for the same football team, have the same number of siblings, even married someone who looks just like the person you married. Spooky, but it's possible. Here's the question, though.

Are they you?

No.

Then why do you want their answers?

No one can give you the answers, because the answers they have are not the answers you need. They can give you guidance and suggestions. They can tell you what worked or didn't for them; but ultimately, the answers you are going to search for and find and keep searching for again are your own. So I hope you didn't come this far in this journey hoping I have all the answers, because if you did, well, the preceding information may be bad, but the following information is going to be even worse.

I don't even have all the answers for myself. Nope. Heck, I don't even have most of them, and the few answers I have are still just works in progress: Because *that is what they will always be.* Nothing in this world is static, why should the answers be. As we grow and change and our world and responsibilities change around us, the questions we need to answer and the answers we've had from before change with it. Who you are now is not who you were half your lifetime ago, and it isn't who you will be twice as many years from now. We change constantly, daily, and we need to be ready for that change to make the best of it. I do have one solid answer, though. There is one answer I found that will never change. It doesn't answer *much*, but it answers *enough* to let the rest of the questions get asked. And since I'm a nice guy, I'm going to share it with you. Not just what it is, but let you have it as well, as the first answer you can use to start with. It's a three-parter, and here it is:

Questions must be asked.
Decisions must be made.
Action must be taken.

(You might recognize those from a certain story earlier in the book.)

Now as you might be able to guess, that's a personal mantra for me. Nothing is going to change in your life without following that very basic blueprint.

Questions must be asked. You can't begin anything until you know what it is you need to begin. This goes back to accepting yourself and realizing the here and now of your situation, what you are unhappy with and what you want to work on.

Decisions must be made. Questions are no good unless there is some resolution to them. This is not to say you need to rush it. I sometimes spend several days mulling over questions I feel that are important and instrumental to helping me move forward. (Of course, if the question is along the lines of "What should I do if this growling bear attacks me?" you may want to work a little quicker on that one.) Once you reach a resolution, one final step remains.

Action must be taken. All of this is no good if the resolution does not result in action. You cannot sit and passive think your life better without marrying it to an action. You can have all the new positive thoughts going on in your mind, but if you still kick puppies, you really haven't changed anything.

You'll notice there's a word missing from all of that. Exactly. The very word that is the title of this chapter, "answer", itself is no part of the answer. "Answer" implies a final thought, and we've already talked about the fact that there is only one big all encompassing final moment in life. The questions that need to be asked are active ones that require both results and activity. If you're reading this, then I'm pretty confident there is one thought, or at least one little family of thought (little thoughts that are interconnected) floating through your mind right now. There's something inside you that is wondering, that's curious, that thinks there is something that's missing, some room for improvement, something along the lines of, "How can I make myself a better person". Maybe you have it focused down to a general quality, something like "better parent", "better spouse", or "better employee". Maybe the question you have is more specific. "How can I quit smoking?" or "How can I have more confidence?" These fit in nicely under the "better person" category. You're searching to improve an area of your life. Any way, it's all fine, as long as you know to resolve the question with a choice that requires action. Answering questions by sitting around a coffee shop at three in the morning answers nothing. It is only an exercise in self indulgence. Trust me.

Resolving questions by finding a result that can be put into practice is what fosters and creates the change that you are looking for. Once that result is found, it then must be turned from an idea into an action. Once you've figured out what it is you need to do, sitting around on the sofa watching Jerry Springer waiting for the activity to come knocking on your door isn't going to cut it. You need to get out there and do it.

And you need to screw it up.

Failure is more than an option.

I know what you're thinking. "What the hell kind of motivation is THAT?!? You WANT me to fail??" No, I don't. Trust me on that one. I want everyone to be successful. I want everyone to see positive results. But I also want everyone to know just what they're up against. You don't <u>need</u> to screw it up, but you better be ready to, because in all likelihood it's going to happen. You know how many failed light bulbs Edison made before he got one that worked? Not every action you take is going to be the one that fits. The one you're taking now, reading this book, this might not even be the right one. But you will never know that if you don't do it. How many times, as a child when presented with something you didn't want to eat, did you tell your parents that you didn't like it? And what would they always say?

"Well, did you try it?"

You'd sulk. "Nooo."

"Well, then how do you know you don't like it?"

For a little bit of full disclosure, that argument never worked on me as a kid. I just dug my heals in deeper and got more and more stubborn and temperamental until I got my way, to the point that when Thanksgiving rolled around, my mom boiled me a couple of hot dogs because she didn't want to hear me scream about hating turkey. I was the pickiest of eaters as a child but you know what funny thing happened along the way to adulthood? Once I was on my own and cooking my own food, I realized that after thirty seven straight days of pasta, I might want to try something else. Now, I eat most anything. There are still foods I avoid, but now I know that they aren't for me. If I never tried it, I never would have developed a taste for seafood and discover that the best fish in the world is Copper River Salmon. Likewise, if I hadn't tried artichokes, I never would have learned that they don't get along with me. The wrong choice is made all the time. If it's wrong, try another one. If that's wrong as well, then choose something else. Or better yet, go back to the question you're asking. Maybe there is a better way to ask it, something more specific, or maybe the focus of the question isn't where it needs to be.

One of the books that I own is called "The Artist's Way." It is a twelve week program helped to artists who feel they have become blocked creatively and give them a new way to focus on their craft. It is a phenomenal program that has literally helped thousands and thousands of people, both through the book as well as workshops that the author Julia Cameron runs. And it doesn't just help artists. People from all walks of life come to her and her teachings for guidance in their everyday lives, to help unblock some of their creativity and live a fuller life. I recommend it to anyone.

Anyone but me, that is.

The book I have is the third copy of it I've owned. I have tried it three times and I have given up three times. Why? Easy. It's not for me. I read the book, it all makes such wonderful sense, I can see where it would be such a fantastic tool, and I try to put it in practice in my life, and I flame out miserably. I think the farthest I ever got into it was week three, but I just never found the completion or progress I was hoping for. I used to get mad at myself, blame myself for it not working. "If it works for everyone else, why not me?" I would scream out. It would leave me feeling worse then when I had started because now not only was I not being as creative as I wanted to be, but also I had failed at the activity that was going to help me become more creative. It took a lot of time and patience for me to realize that it wasn't my fault. It certainly wasn't Ms. Cameron's fault, either. The fact is there is no fault to blame. It was a choice I made and put into action, it didn't work out, so I had to go back and make sure the question I was asking was correct, and then find a new choice that would be more effective. There is still a part of me that wishes it did work for me, that small part that feels left out when everyone else goes to a party and you're stuck working the late shift. The truth is though that not everything works for everyone, and being able to recognize that is what helps a person grow. You go out, you make a choice, you put it in action and you see where it gets you. Maybe it works out maybe it doesn't. What you need to know is that *at least you are in a better place than you were when you started.* How is that possible? Because even though this first choice didn't work out, you know that now. You know that much more about yourself, and it helps to narrow down the list of

61

possible actions. It is not a misstep or a backwards step if something doesn't work out. It is simply part of the learning curve.

Think of yourself as a big block of clay, and inside of that clay is the sculpture of the person you know you can be. How do you go about finding that sculpture? You remove all the clay that isn't part of it. You start taking off corners and smoothing down sides, and in the process maybe you realize you've taken too much off one area and you need to put it back, and there's a spot on the other side that isn't quite right. Maybe you even discover you've taken off too much altogether and you need to put most of it back and start again. So you do it. That's the only way it's going to work. You won't know you've got it right until you've seen it wrong.

There's a great old saying that "Failure is not an option." I suppose in some cases, it isn't, at least not a helpful one. True life-or-death situations come to mind, of course, like rescuing someone from a flood or being involved in a war. I'll grant you that in those situations you probably only have one chance so you better make the best of it. But on a day to day basis, failure is always an option. Not one to strive for, but one that exists: because it needs to. Think of when you learned to ride a bike. I bet you fell a lot. Technically, every time you fell, that was a failure. Now, that doesn't mean you tried once, fell down, and never tried again. Of course not. You picked up your bike and yourself, dusted both off, and tried it again. And each time you fell, you learned a little bit more about balance and coordination and speed until you put it all together and were successful. You can't be afraid to fail, because the only way you can fail is by not doing. And the first step of doing is by asking yourself, "What do I want to do?" Any change in life is just a matter of redefining what you want.

Daylight's wasting

Contrary to what the Rolling Stones tell us, "time" is not on our side. There is probably nothing else in the universe that is as elusive and slippery as time. It is probably easier to find the end of the rainbow than it is to catch up with and control time. There never seems to be enough hours in a day, or days in a week, with the notable exception being the last hours at work before a weekend or the last days before a vacation. Those seem to go on forever. One of my favorite quotes from Einstein addresses just that:

> *When you are courting a nice girl an hour seems like a second. When you sit on a red-hot cinder a second seems like an hour. That's relativity.*

Think about it. Why does a seven day vacation seem to come and go so quickly while a five day work week can sometimes drag on? It is all in our perception of it, and it is this perception that becomes the biggest obstacle: how we view this "time". Every so often I would make a grand plan in my head that I was going to get up every day at the same hour, to start my day productively and positively, and that I would break my old traditions and start new ones, designed to improve me mentally and physically. The problem was I couldn't break the first, most important habit. It is my habit to look at things in negative terms: "I don't want to get up now. I don't need to. I could be sleeping." It never helped that, in taking the time to wake up, there was the struggle against the slumber. Who does not want to just lie there, if even for thirty seconds, when the alarm goes off, contemplating how much nicer it would be to stay there in bed. It would be great if, every morning, I jumped out of bed bright eyed and bushy-tailed, ready to take on the world. The reality is that isn't going to happen until I allow it to by giving it a chance to grow and become part of who I am. There are some mornings when it does happen, and it occurs for a variety of reasons: anticipation over the day's coming events, a good solid night of sleep, dumb luck. But there are certainly more days that are a struggle, sometimes even if you do sleep well and have a great day planned. Think about it. Lying in a nice, snug, warm bed, perhaps curled up next to someone, doing nothing but dreaming. You're supposed to want to give that up voluntarily to get up and go to work? C'mon! But the answer lies in how you look at not just the getting up but the whole day. Once again, it boils down to perspective.

I choose to look at time, elusive as it can be, as a gift I give to myself. The problem is that many people have taken the luxury of that gift away from themselves by cramming it full of "responsibilities" because they feel that they need to. Because of that, now, what downtime most people have is spent in utter passivity, vegging out with the television or video games or what not. I'm not saying that relaxing isn't important, and I'm probably about the last person you'd ever hear advocating something like "Kill your television", but there are ways to be relaxing and stimulating at the same time. The trick is to find that time.

If time is a gift, where do we find it? Maybe for you it is first thing in the morning. Get up an hour earlier tomorrow. You are giving yourself an extra hour to do things for yourself. This is a matter of creating time for yourself, time that you knew existed but just never did anything with. What you do with the time is up to you, and what you think is most needed in your life. Maybe you spend the hour reading, or maybe you used to like to paint and never had the time anymore. Maybe you take up meditation, to help find some focus, or maybe you use the time to exercise. Maybe you spend that hour doing things around the house that you enjoy. I don't know. You probably don't either, but I can tell you this: you're not going to find out unless you get up and do something, anything. Remember, choices must be made and action must be taken, and if it's the wrong action, so be it. You move on.

Okay, so you tried that and after three days of getting up an hour earlier the only thing you've accomplished is generating a burning desire to beat me with my own book. Take it to the flip side. Maybe you're not a morning person. Maybe you're a night owl. So do it then. Take an extra hour at the end of the day. And I don't mean use it just as an excuse to watch Letterman either. Take that time to do something for you, something you feel the need to do. An hour all to yourself.

There is one huge potential problem with all of this, though. The way that society is moving, any more time we spend awake is going to eventually get sucked into outside forces, and the time that you set aside for yourself will be gone. A greater challenge, and perhaps ultimately the more rewarding one, is to not add the hour onto your day, but find the hour within it. Maybe it's the hour when you first come home from work. Maybe it's the hour spent watching crap television because you were killing time between shows you want to watch. Maybe if you're lucky, you have the kind of job that lets you take an hour during the day. Whenever it is, wherever it is, whatever it is for, take it. It's yours.

When I started working on pulling my butt out of the fire as they like to say, I tried to create a set schedule like I always used to. And, like I always used to, I almost immediately started to ignore it. I'm not a structure person to begin with, and to suddenly have a whole new set of rules to follow never sits well, even if I am the one who made up the rules. Now, in the past what would happen would be my getting discouraged by not being able to have success with this new regime and I would give up on it, and the forces that had brought me to the realization that I needed to do something to make a change in my life would simply get that much more control. The unhappiness, the dissatisfaction, the feelings of failure and non-accomplishment would become more galvanized in my system and I would go back to my old ways once again. This time really started out no different. I bought a large desk blotter calendar, pounded a couple of nails (crookedly) in the wall to hang it on, and proceeded to schedule every last minute of my life. I was sure to leave room for notes about how much money I was spending on what and where and how often; what time I was setting aside for myself to write and, most importantly, what time I was getting up in the morning. Come here and take a look at it. Yup, that's right. Seven a.m. Again. Great idea, but here's where it falls apart.

First of all, from the sounds of it, my clothes are going to wash themselves, my apartment will simply never get dirty, and some little gnomes will magically show up at my house once a week with groceries. Secondly, my work schedule, as much as I'd like it to be as immovable as my personal schedule, isn't. (I know what some of you were thinking—"Holy Crap. I want a job that let's me not have to go in until 5 or 6." Sounds nice, but until you know what a close/open is, believe me when I say to you it isn't all peaches and cream.) The joy of being in the restaurant business is that the only thing that is consistent is the inconsistency of it all. Finally, there is this thing called life. People have birthdays that need to be celebrated, doctors have appointments that need to be kept, cars have oil that needs to be changed. Just like my work schedule, my life schedule is always in flux, and to begin to think that I could schedule every last waking moment is absurd. The goal is to find out what works for you. Take a break and look at your life. All of it: work commitments, family commitments, social commitments, everything that takes up space on your schedule every week. You probably do that on a pretty regular basis anyway because you're always trying to squeeze in getting your hair cut, having dinner with the Murphy's, or turning your head and coughing for the nice doctor with the cold hands. But this time don't look at it for those reasons. Look at it and see where that time is. You'll know. You'll recognize time that you waste: time that could be better served. And it isn't necessarily about you. Maybe that time is for you to play catch with your kid, or take a walk with your wife. Or maybe that time is for you to sit down with that old sketch pad from when you dreamt of being the next Rembrandt, or to read that book you've been meaning to finish. Only you will know what you need, but I do know this: The time is there. Go and find it.

Hearing vs. Listening, Knowing vs. Believing, Living vs. Life

I talked about perception very briefly at the top of the last chapter, and how the perception of time seems to fluctuate with how we live our life and what is going on in it. Well, not to get all fourth dimensional, but the fact is that time does fluctuate because that is how we perceive it. Obviously, if we were to sit with a stop watch and time each hour, we would see that they are the same length, but we do not time our lives that statically. We are alive in time and, in accordance to what we are experiencing, time may be too fleeting or too abundant. It comes down to a very simple truth:

Perception is reality. What we perceive is what we experience. Think of an argument you may have had with a person that was based on a misunderstanding. You argue from your position because of your perception of what you consider to be the truth. They counter because they have their own perception. An even better example is a political argument. What is truth in a political ideology? You have your beliefs, I have mine, and every one else has theirs. Surely they can't *all* be the truth. Yet we continue to believe that we are correct and everyone else is wrong. That's perception being reality.

The challenge then becomes to open your perception, and be aware of what reality is. You strive to have a perception that is not created and constrained by the rigidity of your beliefs but a perception based on openness and willingness to grow.

I bring this up because it is an important element to what people believe they have to go through, and what they subject themselves to, in order to be successful in life. We live in a high pressure society, and as such we strive to fit in and keep up, and in doing so, we make concessions in who we are. With our minds focused on expectations, we create roles we try to fill instead of letting ourselves grow as the people we are. We think we need to have the house with the two car garage and the white picket fence. We think we need to maintain a certain level of appearance for the social world we inhabit. We think we need to maintain a constant level of promotion in our career track. In short, we think we need to subscribe to, and achieve, a certain status quo, and in doing so we become *re*-actionary and not *pro*-actionary.

This is not to say that wanting any or all of that stuff is bad. For many people, it's very good. In very stark terms, it is the foundation of our society. Many of us would not have had the upbringing we did if our parents didn't subscribe to that kind of life. But the question I put forth to you right now, and the answer I'm sure I'm going to get, because otherwise you wouldn't be here with me now, is do you want to be a passive person on this journey, or an active one?

When somebody speaks to you, are you actively listening to them and what they have to say, or are you just passively hearing them speak, waiting for it to be your turn? Personally I catch myself more than I'd like to admit already knowing what I'm going to say in response to the other person even before they have finished speaking. How could I really be listening to them and understanding what they are trying to say to me if I already have my answer in mind? By just hearing the sounds and not listening to the words, and just as importantly missing the emotions behind them, we get nothing, we learn nothing. We lose the opportunity to grow and become a richer person for the experience. We have a lesser understanding of what's going on. Another line from the "Desiderata" sums it up perfectly.

Speak your truth quietly and clearly; and listen to others, even the dull and ignorant; they too have their story.

That happens to all of us. We just want the other person to shut up because they can't possibly have anything worthwhile to tell us and that they are just wasting our time. How many times have you been talking to (or more likely, at) someone, you don't think you're making your point, and to ice the cake they say, "I hear what you're saying, and I know what you're talking about" and you want to rip your hair out because they are not doing either of those things? I've even felt the other person thinking that of me, and it paralyzes me and makes me understand how unfair it is to the person you're trying to connect with when I take on the role of the "superior" person. But we do this in order to fulfill the expectation. Once again letting expectation govern how we behave, of who we think we need to be. We don't take the time to be "in the moment" with another person. We simply grab what we think we need as quickly as we can and move on.

When you think about the person you are, how do you see yourself? Do you just say to yourself "This is the person I'm supposed to be"? Or do you really feel inside of you that you are the person you want to be? We all grow up knowing what we are supposed to do. Many people let that become the sole guiding force in their life. They do what they know, but do they do what they believe?

A kid I grew up with has a father who is a lawyer. Kid probably always knew he was going to be a lawyer. No reason not to be. The father was very successful and well liked and respected in his practice, and the kid was certainly intelligent and outgoing with a very engaging personality. Not only did he know he was going to be a lawyer, but he probably just as certainly knew he was going to go into business with his father.

Funny thing happened on the way to what he knew. He found something he believed. I remember him talking to me about it. I was finishing up college, he was almost done with law school and we just happened to run into each other out and about when he told me his plans. He was going to be a lawyer all right. In fact he already had a job lined up for when he passed the bar. Only it wasn't with his dad. It was with the public defender's office. This was almost fifteen years ago. I saw him not too long ago. He's still doing it, and he still enjoys it. He is still doing what he believes.

To believe something is to be able to not just accept something but to own it and defend it without having any empirical evidence that it is true. I know that two plus two equals four. I know this because I can have two apples and you can give me two more and, ta da, I have four apples. I believe people, if given the opportunity, are at their core good people. What proof do I have? Well, I can relate anecdotes and show examples, but ultimately there is no test that can be done, no double blind study with a control group, no nothing that can give me the facts that shows my belief to be true. And yes, I've been taken advantage of by people because of that belief, but I still believe it, because it is part of who I am and not just something I know.

How often are you asked on a daily basis what you believe? What you know is almost always being called upon, whether it is at work or at home or wherever, and we can spout out what we know. (Like I said, I'm a mean Trivial Pursuit player.) As such, what we know becomes more important than what we believe. We lose sight of what is inherently part of us because we feel the obligation to place more emphasis on simply what we know and not what we believe.

The perception is we think we have to be a certain type of person, and that becomes our reality. The outcome of this is that we are living, but we are barely having a life. We hear what we have to, and we know what we are supposed to, but we never listen to what we need to and we never believe like we should.

The reality is we need to stop and listen, and we need to stand up and believe. Without being aware of who we are and what we believe in, we have no way of understanding how it is we are supposed to grow. And without being able to listen, not just what other people are saying to us but to everything around us and to ourselves, and really take it in, we have no way to begin growing, to begin becoming the person we believe ourselves to be.

It's easier than you think

There are lots of little quotes I keep taped around my desk to help keep me motivated. One of them is something I cobbled together from some things I've read over the years, specifically from some Eastern philosophy texts:

What is right may not be easy
What is wrong may not be hard
What is hard may not be right
What is easy may not be wrong

It is not to choose between what is hard and what is easy;
It is to choose between what is right and what is wrong.

That is one of the most important and yet most overlooked parts of this, of any work one does that is of a personal nature. It doesn't necessarily have to be difficult to be effective, and that is something that runs so counter to how most of us have been raised that it almost doesn't make sense. How many times have you heard someone say "That can't be right, it was too easy"? It is drilled into our brains that anything that needs to be done is going to be challenging and a struggle, and anything that comes easy to us can't be good for us. That is probably true for the most part. If all good things came easy to us, we wouldn't have such a hard time doing them. Also you wouldn't need to be reading this. Some do, most don't, and we work on those that are hard in order to reach success with ourselves.

The trick is not to be confused with what we should be focusing on. It isn't whether something is hard or easy that should be the basis for our decision. It is whether it is good or bad, in the long run, and these are decisions we make a hundred times a day, even if we're not always aware of it.

I hate to go to the grocery store. I really do. I know that even with a list, I'm still not going to be sure what to get, and I know that when I get it home, I'm not always going to want to cook it. As such, I've managed to really pare down what I eat. Things that involve the least amount of time and dishes get priority. Problem is I took that too far.

It is easy to go to the grocery store, and it is relatively easy to make most of what I buy, but you know what is easier? Swinging through the drive thru at McDonald's or walking down the block to the Subway sandwich shop on the corner. So, what's the right decision?

I have a soft spot for Mickey D's, and Jared tells me that Subway is good for me, but I know that the money I can spend at those places in two days will buy me groceries for a week. That won't be much comfort when I'm hungry and realize it's going to take me thirty or forty five minutes to make a meal, more than enough time to go out, buy something and be finished, but it'll be comfortable to know that I'm eating healthier, taking better care of my body, and not trivially wasting money. But that is not a one time decision, to go to the grocery store or not. It is a decision I make every time I'm hungry, because there are lots of good take out places in the neighborhood.

That's the joy of life. It is never a matter of "I'm going to. . ." and it just magically happens, never having to be addressed again. It is a continual series of decisions, most having to be faced every day, and it is how we deal with them.

Notice how I said deal with them. I didn't say agonize over them. We, as a society, have gotten to a point where every little decision we make is a life or death one. Don't believe me? Go to your local golf course and hang around one of the greens. These guys will take five minutes lining up a three foot putt as if the PGA Championship is riding on the balance. (And when they inevitably miss it they both: A) curse like a sailor, and B) blame something other than themselves. It's actually pretty funny, if you're not stuck in the foursome behind them.) The moral of the story is that we wind ourselves up so tight on the simplest of questions that we lose sight of what it is we're trying to figure out. This ties back in with the whole "Don't be surprised if you fail once in a while". Once again I'm not telling you to try and fail. I'm saying you're going to be more successful if you just back off and trust yourself a little bit more. Some right decisions will be hard. Going back to school after many years off? Hard. You're out of the habit of studying, you need to juggle your schedule around, you're the oldest person in class. (Some people have told me that being the oldest is the hardest part, feeling out of place from everyone else.) Ninety nine times out of a hundred it's the right decision to make, but some of the reason it's hard is because you (drum roll, please) *EXPECT* it to be hard. (There's that word again.) Once you get into it, and start the routine of it, you may turn to yourself and say "Wow, this is so much easier than I thought it was going to be." Many paths are hard only because we make them hard in our minds. We build them up to be these impenetrable walls that we are forced to break through, only to find out when we get to the other side they were nothing more than paper maché and chicken wire. That is why you can not look at your options and say "That's the harder one so that must be the right one." You need to look at them and say "That is the right one to do."

What makes the right decision seem harder some times is the fact that, unfortunately, the right decision in this day and age is the different one, the decision that sets you apart from everyone else, and nobody likes to be that person. I may be dating myself here, but I remember a time before there was mandatory recycling. The easy thing to do would be of course just to throw everything into the garbage cans, drag them to the street once a week and watch the landfill pile up. But if you wanted to make the effort, you would rinse out your cans and bottles, being sure to separate the glass by color (this was the old days, kids) and keep the old newspapers separate as well. Then every Saturday while Mom was doing laundry you get into the van with your Dad and your older brother and drive down to the dump and (this was the best) throw the bottles into their respective bins and watch them shatter and smash before throwing the newspapers into their receptacle and going on our way. Now, by definition, it was harder than just throwing it all out, but it certainly didn't seem any harder, and judging by what's become the norm over the last thirty years, it was the right thing to do. And we didn't sit there every Saturday morning saying "Woe is me! I can not decide! Should I make the effort or just collapse under the weight of these options?" We just did it. It wasn't an agonizing decision.

Yes, there are many decisions that are heavier than others. Do I marry this person? Do I take this job? Do I pull the plug? Some decisions require time and guidance and patience. They will be wrestled with and, unfortunately, probably carried with you long after the decision has been made. But when you find yourself in a not so life or death situation struggling to decide, stop and ask yourself: is it really that important? Do you really need to be stressing yourself out, tying yourself in knots, bringing everything else in your life to a halt just to decide? Take a deep breath, really think about it, recognize it for what it is, and you'll realize that it's easier and more right than you think.

The Optometrist of Life
(or "Which is better, number one or number two?")

Every time you go to the eye doctor, the same thing happens. You sit in the chair, he starts flipping the lenses back and forth, and then begins that optometrist mantra. "Which is better, number one or number two? Number two or number three? Number two or number four? Number four or number five? Number five or number one?" Honestly, I'm amazed I get a prescription even close to what I need, because by the time he gets to numbers six and seven, I already forgot how good or bad number one or two might have been. Then when he shows me, I can never decide. Do I like number one because it's definitely better, or am I just partial to it because it's the first one I saw? And is there really that much difference between number two and number five? In a perfect world, he'd let me take that whole contraption home for the day and use it in real life, so I could come back the next day and say "Number two was really good when I was driving, but when I was at work, my left eye liked number six while my right eye was fond of number seven, and we found that number nine was great for reading but not so much for television, which was more like number four. Make me that pair." But that little two minute experiment is the foundation to building a successful life. By constantly seeing what works better in our life, we come closer to finding a sustainable balance.

Notice I didn't say perfect balance. That phrase is the bane of my existence. I honestly believe that phrase is the one thing that stands between me and total enlightenment/cosmic happiness/universal truth or whatever you want to call it. Not because it exists, but because I am obsessed with it. I am firmly convinced that it is possible to achieve perfect balance in life. Intellectually I know it'll never happen, but that doesn't stop me from trying for it. There is a difference, however, between striving for perfection and expecting perfection.

To strive for perfection is simply another way of saying that you are going to try to do something better than you did it before.

Whether it is as simple as tie your shoelaces to as noble as how you lead your life, it is all just about making that forward progress. An easy way to look at it, a little affirmation I find myself saying at odd times during the day, just to make sure my head is still screwed on straight, is "I'm going to do better today than I did yesterday, and I am going to do better tomorrow than I did today." That helps me in two ways. First it gives me the positive attitude I need to improve in whatever way I can over yesterday, and secondly, it grounds me in the reality that no matter how I do today, tomorrow I will have the chance to do even better. Doctors don't perform brain surgery on their first day of med school. (At least I hope not.) They spend years and years studying, learning, practicing, understanding everything it takes to perform the surgical task required. Then when they are ready, they assist others to see first hand, learning from them. Finally they take all their learning and skill and put it into practice. That is striving for perfection.

Expecting perfection would be walking into med school on the first day and demanding a patient and a scalpel, thinking you can do it all. It's not going to happen. Perfection, like everything else in this world, is fluid. Don't believe me? Get a hold of some old tapes of figure skating and gymnastics and watch the athletes. You will see some of them get perfect scores. Now watch some from this era. You will see harder maneuvers performed more capably and yet lower scores will be awarded. Why? The idea of what is perfect moves on and changes with everything else. One thing you need to understand if you want any hope of making it through this world with a smile on your face is this:

There is no such thing as perfection.

I'll pause for a minute for the requisite gnashing of the teeth and pounding of the fists that usually accompanies me making that statement. It's a tough thing to swallow, because people get too wrapped up in the "all or nothing" belief. They think there has to be perfection, because if there isn't, then what's the point of trying at all? The point is the trying. It's like the old saying: hard work is its own reward. There is a motto I heard once that stuck with me, from an international organization that literally helps millions of people a year, and it goes like this:

"Let me win. If I cannot win, then let me be brave in the attempt."

We all want to win. It's the American way. But win is a tough word, because too many people focus on the other side of it. If someone wins, that means someone else has to lose. So either you're beating somebody else, you're comparing yourself with others and taking pride in them being less successful then you, or somebody else is beating you, and instead of focusing on where you might have done better, you worry about the other person and concern yourself with beating them the next time.

Let me tell you something. You aren't in competition with anyone but yourself. The only person you have to beat, to be better than, is yourself because the only person that is better than you is the person inside you that you know you have the potential to be. You're not trying to "win" a race with anyone else. When you are making strides to get better in your own life, to recapture the magic of who you were once were or who you want to be, it is only you that you have to worry about. Remember when I said no one had your answers because no one else is you? If they're not you, then they're not trying to do the same things you are, and therefore they're not your competition. The race is only with you. So don't think of win as half of win/lose. Think of win as trying to move ahead from where you have been. And if you don't win today, don't let it be because you felt like not doing anything. Let it be because you tried, you made the effort, and where it brought you wasn't where you needed to go. You asked the question, you made the choice, you went into action, and it didn't work out. Ask the question again, and try a new action. Remember, better person today than yesterday, better person tomorrow than today.

So, if we can accept that there is no such thing as perfection, then it is an easy step to accept that a "perfect" balance is impossible. Sure, it's easy to stand on your own two feet and say to yourself, in the relative ease and quiet of your own room, that you will find that perfect balance, but as soon as you leave that room and step out into the real world, you will see where that all falls apart. Or better yet, stay standing right there in the room and imagine this:

Life is not one thing. It is a multitude of things that you must keep an eye on. In other words, you're juggling. You're juggling your job and all of the responsibilities that come with that (That's got to be two or three balls at least). You're juggling your family (one ball per person, please). You're juggling the joys of life

(Mortgage? One ball. Car payments? That's another. Utilities? One for each bill.) Not to mention any other things in your life, you know, hobbies, social clubs, church, PTA, you get the picture. You got twenty or thirty balls you're trying to juggle and what's best is you're not the only one juggling them. All those work balls you're juggling? Everyone you're working with is juggling the same ones, so you don't even know when it's going to be your turn to have it and how long you can get it for. Hell, your boss might think your pretty good and throw another ball at you just to see if you can handle it. And all those family balls you got in the air? You got it. Your family's got them too. So, now you're not only trying to juggle all of these, you need to find a way to juggle them with everyone else, and we're not even done yet.

You see, we haven't talked about all of the outside events that you have no control over but have a bearing on you. Snowstorm comes out of nowhere, car breaks down unexpectedly, the economy crashes, you can not influence any of these things enough to be in charge of them but they have no problem screwing up your life big time. So, imagine not that you are standing flat foot on the floor, but rather on a teeter board that is balanced on a ball that is lying in a pool of extra slippery grease. Go ahead, zippy. Find the perfect balance in that.

Life isn't something you can force. It happens the way it happens and all you can do is adapt the best you can. Let's go back to that image. Juggling aside, there is no way you could stand on a teeter board in a pool of grease and have it stand stock still. But what you can do is learn to move with it when it does. You feel it rolling one way, you simply shift your weight the other way, try to bring it back a little. You're always going to be moving. The trick is to find the way that has you moving in harmony. That is the balance you are looking for.

You can do anything you want. You just can't do it today.

There's a classic "Dear Ann Landers" column from many, many years ago that has always stuck with me for what you will see is a pretty obvious reason. A woman writes in saying that she's thinking about making a change in her life, but that to do so she'll have to go back to school, and to get the schooling she needs it's going to take her five years, and by then she'll be forty, and what should she do.

Ann's response?

"How old are you going to be five years from now if you don't go back to school?"

That is such a simple and eloquent way to illustrate what is such a stumbling block for so many people. Many people actually possess the desire for change. They recognize that there is a bigger way to live and that they wouldn't mind doing it, if it didn't take so long. This woman wants to improve her life. She sees the opportunity to advance herself by doing something that interests her, but that all gets overshadowed by the length of time that such a commitment is going to take. Granted, her question partially originated from a place of fear. 'What if I do all this and it doesn't work out?' is certainly going through her mind, but the greater issue at stake here is that she is saying 'This is something I want now. I don't want to have to wait five years for it.' And this was from way before we had the instant gratification world of the internet and PDA's. Ann's response says 'If this is what you want to do, this is the time it's going to take. And if you do it, I promise you at the very least you will be no worse off then than you are now. And if you don't do it, those five years are still going to go by, and then all you'll have to show for it is regret for not taking the chance.'

Think about something you've always wanted to do but haven't ever thought was possible in the realm of human experience. (In other words, if the phrase "Time Travel" is going through your mind, pick something else.) Now, unless you picked something screamingly mundane like boil water, it's probably not something you can do right this second. Still want to do it? Great, let's get started.

Two examples already mentioned in the book couldn't have less in common as activities, but both can be used to serve the illustration. We'll start with the less life threatening one, bowling. It is certainly something easy to get started, in the sense that most anyone with about five bucks and some mode of transportation can get to a bowling alley, rent the shoes, pick up a ball and roll it at the pins. But that doesn't make you a bowler.

Even if you spend all day at the lane, success isn't going to come in a day at this. There are techniques to learn, such as how to and when to throw a hook, how to pick up a spare, the scoring system, why does this lane seem more oily than that lane, I never knew I had muscles in that part of my back, and all sorts of other fun stuff that Norm Duke and Walter Ray Williams make look so easy. (Go ahead and google them. I'll wait.) I guarantee that if you've never bowled before in your life and you go out and play three games, you will have a muscle soreness running from the shoulder of your dominant arm diagonally across your back. Bowling is a lot like many other things in this world. It takes a minute to learn and a lifetime to master. At the end of the day you aren't going to say "Hey world, look at me! I'm a bowler!!" But if you want to be able to say that, then you're going to have to spend some time practicing.

There is a very simple theory behind all of this. Time plus commitment equals success. What makes it simple is that half of the equation is a constant. Time doesn't change. Five years will be five years whether you spend it being productive or not. What you bring to it is the commitment to be successful at what it is you want to do and what level of success you are looking to achieve. It is possible that with only a few times practicing you would be good enough to consider yourself a competent bowler, comfortable enough if a friend said "Hey, let's go bowling tonight" you wouldn't worry about looking foolish. A few months of practice and some research, maybe buying your own shoes or trying a few different types of balls, and you may feel confident enough to join a league. How long would it take to be ready to think about being a professional? Well, that's up to you and your commitment. How much time are you willing to spend, what kind of life are you willing to accept to make it happen, how much natural aptitude do you have? Maybe it doesn't take long, or maybe it takes longer than you think. The good thing with bowling, or any other activity that is being done strictly as a hobby, is that there is always a point at which a person can say "This is enough for me." They reach a level of comfort with it and how it fits into their life, and that's where it stays.

Brain surgery, however, does not fall into the hobby category. I have heard of bridge clubs, dart leagues and knitting circles, but I have never heard of a brain surgery social. In other words, if you wake up some day and say "I think I'll be a brain surgeon" you ain't pussy footing around.

I made the reference before that brain surgeons don't (hopefully) start cutting up on patients the first day they go to med school. Mostly I'm sure that's due to insurance liabilities, but another part of it to consider for the sake of this argument is that when a person decides they want to be a brain surgeon, they have a whole lot to do *even before they start brain surgery training.*

First of all there is the whole undergraduate experience known as pre-med. Then there is the whole med school, followed by that lovely time known as being a surgical intern. Then, and I'll fully admit this last part is just speculation, there's probably a whole extra special internship with just neurosurgery. So off hand, what do you think we're looking at? Ten years, maybe twelve. That's a commitment. But there is obviously a reason for that.

Our heads are not just cans of spaghetti-o's a person can "pop" open with a can opener. They need to know where it all is, what it all does and how to put it all back the way it's supposed to be. AND they have to be able to do that without thinking too much about the fact that they literally have someone else's life in their hands. I'm almost thinking that if I'm going in for brain surgery and the doctor comes up to me says "Don't worry. I'm so good I finished my studies in half the time it normally takes." I might just say "Great, but I'll take the guy who took his time to be sure he knew everything."

With a vocation, unlike a hobby, there is no jumping off early point. Yes, at some point you have learned enough to begin doing what it is you want to be doing, but the learning curve does not stop there. There is always more to learn, there are always ways to better yourself. Am I saying that it is more important to focus on improving your job-life than it is your social-life? For some base societal reasons, it is, the most practical being that one provides for you the basic needs for survival. But a very good way to look at it from a mental and emotional standpoint is that one provides for living, and another provides for life. That's a conversation for a later chapter. What is important here is the understanding on how this affects how you live.

I met a friend of a friend at a party one night. Neither one of us really knew anyone else so we started talking between ourselves. He's an intense and intelligent person and the conversation was very invigorating when he stopped me cold with one question.

"How does it feel," he asked me, "to know that you could do anything you want?"

I'm sure I came out with something witty and pithy, about how I already knew that and the biggest challenge I had was figuring out what it was that I wanted to do, but he wasn't buying it, so he asked me again.

How does it feel to know that you could do anything you want?

We talked on further about it and I don't know what I said, but I know I defended it vigorously, such was I at the time, still convinced that I knew everything. "I have lived!" I screamed out in the subtext of my arguments. "I have studied acting in New York! I have lived in San Francisco! I have buried a parent! I have lived! What could you possibly have to teach me?" Such was the incredulity of my conceit. Here I was presented with an opportunity to learn, to open my mind, and I dismissed it with flippancy. I know he understood the stubbornness that I was camouflaging in empty knowledge and wisdom, so he let it go, but with a sly little smile on his face that someday, I would understand what he was trying to tell me. I'm sure the only thing that kept me from smacking that smile off his face was, somewhere inside, I knew he was right.

You CAN do anything that you want. That's the part you bring to the equation. What is it that you want to do? The time is there. The time is always there, moving on. And whether you do or not, time will. And if you want to do something but you won't because you can't do it in one day, guess what? Tomorrow will come and you still won't be able to do then either.

Dream while you're asleep; Visualize while you're awake.

Someone once wrote in to *Playboy* magazine to complain. Not about the naked pictures, but that the articles they wrote on travel and fashion and home electronics were all about things that were priced much out of the range of the average person that read the magazine, and why would they do that? Surely it makes more sense and be less condescending to include articles about things they could actually afford. *Playboy's* response, in so many words, was "We don't write about the life you have. We write about the life you wish you had." Great way to run a magazine. Not so hot a way to live your life.

Dreams are an inherently important part of the human experience, but they can start to become a problem if we spend too much time focused on the dream and not enough time on the reality. (And just to be sure we're all clear here I'm talking about day dreams, fantasies, whatever you want to call them. The dreams we have at night are a whole different animal. No less important in my mind, but they serve a vastly different purpose.) If you spend too much time focused on the dream, it eventually becomes a person's nature to expect the dream to come true. That is why I say dream at night, but visualize when you are awake. There may be a small difference between those two words in the dictionary, but there is a huge difference in how they affect your life.

Dreams are passive activities, most commonly brought about by a desire created in response to a negative situation. You wake up and realize it is twenty degrees, so you dream about going somewhere tropical on a vacation. Your boss is harassing you about a project at work, so you dream about winning the lottery and never having to work again. Your car needs to go into the shop and while you wait for the repairs you dream of driving something brand new and luxurious. These are all good distractions for a very short period of time, but if they become the way you live your life, eventually they stop being distractions and start becoming something you're going to take for granted. Eventually it becomes "Why does it always have to be so cold? Can't I live somewhere warm?" "I'm tired of having to work all the time. Can't I just be rich?" "Why can't I have a really nice car that doesn't give me problems?"

You've gone from dreaming about something to whining about something. You've done nothing to help make these dreams come true, and instead you have only served to make yourself more bitter about the life you are leading, and, worst of all, you have only helped to pull yourself farther out of the present moment and place and will only continue to reinforce the negative aspects of how you are living.

Visualization is an active pursuit. You take the time to truly imagine what the result will be. You view the positive outcome that you are looking for. And most importantly, you engage your whole system to make it happen that way.

When you engage the whole system, the whole system works to make it happen. Sitting on your sofa day dreaming about the tropics doesn't get you there. With your system actively engaged, you begin to flesh out what it is you're looking for. Do you want to move somewhere, or just take a vacation there? What kind of experience are you looking for? What is it going to take to make that happen? These are all parts of the whole solution. What makes it different, and ultimately something that is successful in happening, is that when all of you is present in this, you begin to understand the parameters surrounding it. You will recognize that, although you may be able to create the image of yourself lounging in a hammock while beautiful, half naked island natives feed you grapes all day, there is a reality that you will take into consideration, sometimes consciously, sometimes subconsciously. (Don't believe me? Get that image in your mind of you in the hammock and the natives feeding you. Know how I know it's not going to happen? The person you're picturing in the hammock looks way more like Brad Pitt or Angelina Jolie than it does you. That's why it's called a fantasy.) Your system as a whole, your physical, your mental, and your emotional all slowly work together to figure out if this is something that can happen, to what extent it can happen, and most importantly how to make it happen when you are ready for it.

You realize it's just a vacation that you want, so you start to research when airfares are cheapest and if there are package deals you can work out. You find yourself spending less discretionary income so you can have more money for the trip. You find yourself reading the travel section more and talking to friends who have been on similar vacations. You decide to walk the three flights instead of taking the elevator because you know you're going to be wearing nothing but shorts in a month. All these little things start to come together, but none of them would ever begin if you didn't do the all important first step to making anything happen:

Visualizing what it is you want to achieve.

I know, I know I can hear you now calling shenanigans on me. "How is visualizing something any different than creating an expectation for something?" They are as different as night and day. An expectation is a hard and fast object, no exceptions. A visualization is the road map we help create for ourselves as we go on our journey. An expectation is an outcome of the passivity of a dream. It's almost like a math equation:

I am cold. Being cold makes me unhappy. I dream of being warm. Therefore, if I go somewhere warm, I expect to be happy, because I will no longer be cold.

It's that simple, it's that cut and dried. Visualization creates the life inside of us that creates the possibility to reach our goals. It is an ever changing thing, constantly being tuned and tweaked as we discover the ways to make it happen. We learn that if we decide that we need to be somewhere warmer, there are many other aspects of our lives that are going to change. The work we do may have to be different, the social life we have will disappear and a new one will be created, the opportunities and environment in which we live will necessitate changes in how we live our lives. Ultimately, where we end up may be a much different place than what we first visualized. In constantly fine tuning it and going back to it and letting us guide it as much as it guided us, we will have reached a place of contentment and happiness. Whereas if we just said, "I'm going somewhere I expect to be warm" and just left it at that, our lives would be even emptier than before we made the change, because we did not let the journey happen organically.

Think of it this way. You're reading this book because you've decided that you want to be a better father. What do you think is going to be more successful? Sitting around saying to yourself "I expect to be a better father" and thinking that's going to change anything? Or taking the time to visualize what it means to you to be a better father? Maybe your first reaction is that you need to help them more with their homework, but you never had the time, or you were afraid that you wouldn't be able to help them. So you start to work with that, rearranging your schedule, studying what they're studying. You do this, and you start to notice that your time with them is always spent authoritatively and never in a more relaxed setting, so you play more games with them, or take them out to the movies once in a while. (And you will to start to notice things. The more you open yourself up to what you are actively working on, the more you will be able to see and feel). The visualization becomes part of the journey. It is part of the path with you, helping you find new ways to navigate.

One last example. Go to the batting cages and get two tokens. For the first one, I want you to stand there and "expect" to hit the ball. Do nothing else (well, obviously swing at some point) but say to yourself before every pitch "I expect to hit this ball" and see how you do. Then get ready to put the second token in, but before you do, close your eyes and "visualize" hitting the ball, and all that goes into it, the timing, the different parts of your body that you use, everything. Then drop the token in and get ready. And after every pitch, do another quick visualization. You will find that, without having to try, your body will respond with what didn't happen right the first time. Your visualization will change little by little, perhaps even imperceptibly while you adjust to what you need to do.

If you expect to hit the ball**, your body will be static, and it will not make the adjustments it needs to. If you visualize hitting the ball, your system will respond, and the visualization will change with you as you strive to be better at hitting the ball. That's the difference. An expectation is a mental creation that we keep outside of ourselves and constantly focus on instead of what we are doing and how we are living in the present. A visualization is an organic part of who we are, kept in all parts of our system, and journeys with us to help guide us on the path we want to be on. You can see why one is such a hindrance that we need to be rid of it forever and the other is almost a necessity in keeping us both grounded and focused: at the same time helping us grow and blossom.

**By the way, if you're reading this and your name is Albert Pujols, skip the batting cage exercise. We all know you can hit.

What ties you down is what gives you roots.

One of the challenges to living an improved life is that we are not purely and wholly rational objective creatures. From time to time we can be, or at least more objective than we normally are (and to be sure some people have mastered the art of being so objective most of the time that it borders on objectionable) but as a rule we let our emotions into our thought and decision making process. Don't believe me? I can put it in very stark terms for you. I bet that when a close family member of yours that you loved dies, your first thoughts were not about how much insurance they had and how you didn't have to travel to see them anymore. Harsh, yeah, but it is a perfect example of how emotion and subjectivity are part of our governing forces.

To add to that is the fact that if you are looking to improve your life, to do something better with yourself, you are answering an emotional longing from inside of you. There are certainly some areas of improvement that have a rational side to them, "If I become a better golfer, I can play professionally and make more money than I do now." but most of the improvements we make in our lives do not have bench marks we can compare ourselves to or a list to fill out to know we are successful. You want to be a better parent? You'll only know you're on the right track by the way your kids respond to you. You want to be a non-smoker? You can certainly judge your process by the number of days you go without smoking, but I'm pretty sure the reason you quit in the first place wasn't just so you'd have something to count. And since part of our nature is to be subjective and emotional, the ability to accomplish something we set out to do is much compromised if we are not emotionally invested in doing it. It is much harder to put effort behind something we simply think than it is something we feel.

We take this subjectivity, we include the heightened emotional life we have that brings us to this point of wanting to improve something in our lives, and we add to that the inherent fear and hesitation we naturally feel when facing change, and we create a new set of obstacles to overcome: the "if only's". "I would do this, if only I didn't have to take care of my family." "I would be a much better husband, if only I didn't have such a stressful job." And these "if only's" don't necessarily need to be things you view negatively. You might love both your family and your stressful job, but without meaning to, you are selling them short and offering up the excuse that "if only you weren't so tied down", you'd be a much better person.

It isn't what ties you down. It's what gives you roots.

We all have things in our lives that are necessary. They are simply part of the balancing/juggling act I talked about before. We can't do anything about getting rid of them. We can certainly improve on them, we can find ways to handle them more efficiently, we might even be able to combine a couple here and there, but they are always going to be with us, so we might as well make the best of it. The first step in doing so is the easiest thing to do. It's the perception we allow ourselves to have.

Just think of the images to start. I look at the phrase "to be tied down" and I instantly get the image of Gulliver from "Gulliver's Travels" when he has been captured by the Lilliputians and is criss-crossed in rope from head to toe and staked to the ground. Impossible to move even, no ability to break free, unable to do anything to help himself, he is stuck. (Some of you may get another image when thinking about being tied down. I hope you have a safe word.) But the image "to have roots" brings to mind a tall huge oak tree, firm and solid in its foundation and as such able to grow to amazing heights and spread its limbs far and wide. Because is it rooted, it is given the opportunity to become all that it always had the potential for. And if something that is smaller than a golf ball has the ability to grow into a mighty oak tree simply because it has taken root, what kind of growth do you think a person like you could have if given the same opportunity?

So don't say to your self "I am tied down." Say "I am rooted." Does your family tie you down with obligations and commitments? Or do they give you roots with their love and their humor, their support and their care? It is easy for us to see the negative in life, easily expressed through a huff or an eye roll when a change is made in the plans and you say to yourself, "Now I have to take care of this, too." And yet when given the opportunity to think about the positive, the good memories from a trip taken together, or just the simple laughing that may occur over the dinner table, we take these things for granted. This is what we *expect* to happen as a family, and so we don't give it the proper respect it deserves. So change it with one simple thing.

Every time you think about that which you believe ties you down, make the effort to follow it up by thinking "That's what gives me roots to grow." What are we talking here, three seconds, maybe four? Even if you do that fifty times a day, and you're a slow thinking (five seconds), that's a grand total of just over four minutes out of your life. It's the easiest thing to do and, if you're still feeling embarrassed about people knowing you're trying something different in your life, nobody's going to know you're doing it (unless you're one of those people whose lips move when they are thinking to themselves). Make a song out of it, set it to music, make it rhyme somehow, whatever you have to do to make it something that quickly becomes not something you think about but is just an organic part of who you are. Soon it will become more than natural. It will become a truth that your system accepts as part of itself, and the platform you have for growth has just become infinitely wiser.

But remember Spiderman's uncle: ***"With great power comes great responsibility."***

You've learned to take root, to see what you have in your life as positive assets and you have grown in wonderful and tremendous ways. You look back at the person you used to be and you laugh at yourself, thinking of how far you've come, and before you know it, you go too far. Your ego and pride, inflated by this great sense of accomplishment, clouds your vision and you forget what it is that gave you that strength, that opportunity. You need to help foster that support so that your roots will continue to be strong. You need to nurture that support in the very same others who nurtured it in you, otherwise those that set you free will ultimately let you drift.

What's the title of this book?

Exactly. There is no self help. Although the journey you go on to make improvement is one ultimately guided by the path you are looking for, it is never a journey we are on alone. We draw on strength and support from so many others, but it is also our responsibility to return that support to them, and to nurture their own strength in them. There is an old saying, that a rising tide lifts all boats. As we grow, as we become better people, we can not selfishly horde that energy inside of ourselves. It does nothing inside of us. It can not grow. We need to be sure that it is spread throughout. Only as it is given out to others through our positive actions and beliefs can it multiply so that it is there for everyone to grow from.

Our job ties us down, but if we change our belief, we see it as a place to root us and give us the chance to grow, and we do. We approach our work with a positive attitude, it feeds on itself, we not only like out job more but we also do our job better. We increase our skills, we improve our standing, this energy flows through all parts of our life and we become the better more positive person we envisioned. And to this job that gave us that support, we return to it that positive growth, we feed it as it fed us and it spreads like a . . . well, the first two things that spread that come to mind are "cancer" and "fungus", and neither one of those exactly pops with positivity . . . so we'll say it spreads like sunshine breaking through the clouds after a heavy rain. It slowly reaches everywhere, illuminating all things and fostering in them the same growth and strength in them that it did in you.

Some of you may be feeling left out. You may be thinking "But I live too much like you did Jack. I've traveled a lot, I've been all over, I don't have the luxury of family close by or a steady job to draw from. How can any of this help me?" It can, with two very important distinctions.

Distinction number one is that it is possible to have your roots in the road. It is just as easy to draw strength and support from the energy that is present everywhere in the world as it is to draw it from one stable spot. It is very much from my travels that I have become the person I am, and have found within me the strength to see the more positive way to live. It is from the places I've lived, the jobs I've had and the people I've met that I have become rooted in this world and able to grow to my potential. And part of that leads to distinction number two.

In this world, it isn't just about friends and families as we look for ways to find our roots. It is also from O.P.L.U.'s.

Other Person Like Us

When we are looking for others to accept us, to understand us and support us as we grow in this world, there is a level of natural selection that comes into play. If you are trying to become a better airplane mechanic, for instance, you are probably not going to surround yourself with friends that are Amish. You want and need someone or ones that are more compatible to what you are going through. Sometimes you look for them, but more often than not they simply just seem to turn up in your life. In Key West, two such people literally walked into my bar.

I don't know if I'm like you. I look at the people I choose to spend my time with and the majority of them, probably something in the ninetieth percentile, are people I have known for ten years or more. For whatever reason, it has been hard for me to meet people in the more recent past that have stayed with me. I know that much of that has to do with the fact that I have moved around a lot, and by a lot, I mean twenty plus addresses in the last seventeen years in at least four different cities. To be fair, in all of my moves I have met wonderful people who were the mainstays in my life at the time, and if I were to run into them again, I can all but guarantee that we would have a fantastic time catching up. How much of a friendship would exist beyond that shared memory is hard to gauge. People change, times change, what was important back when we spent time together isn't the same things now, and I don't hold that against anybody. It doesn't take away from what our friendship was; it just puts it in perspective for what it is.

This is where this story becomes an anomaly of sorts. This couple stopped in, had a couple of drinks, and in the course of the conversation, I learned that they were not just two tourists here for a week, but two people who had just moved to town. They worked for a company that gave them the leeway to work from wherever, and they decided to take advantage of that. They came back in a week later and, like a good bartender, I remembered what they drank. (If I was a great bartender, I would have remembered their names, but as

I have demonstrated earlier in this work, my memory ain't what it should be.) Over the course of several visits we became friends, and then good friends. How good? That year, 2005, four hurricanes hit Key West. The first one, Dennis, I rode out at my apartment. By the time the second one, Katrina, came through, I had already been invited to ride it out with them, and when hurricanes three and four, Rita and Wilma respectively, came calling, they had already asked me to move in. They had more space than they needed. They lived right down town, whereas, I lived out in what is called mid-town. Most importantly, we were good enough friends that we all knew it would be a good idea.

The house that we shared was a beautiful little old conch house that had a fantastic back yard that was half patio/half wild forest. The vegetation grew so thick that it was almost completely private. Case in point: There was an outdoor shower, an invention which I absolutely love, that I had no problem using completely naked, because I knew no one else could see me. (It was especially fun to be using that when you heard the "Conch Tour Train"--the tourist special that drove them around showing the sights—would roll by not twenty feet away. I always wanted to run out and give them a memory to take back home to Kansas.) There was a little fish pond that sat on the edge of the patio, and we rigged up a misting system that would keep us cool no matter how hot the day would get. We would sit out there for dinner, or cocktails before (or after) a night of hitting the town. It was out there that we would get to know each other, telling the stories about who we were and how we ended up where we had been in our lives. Much like sitting around a coffee shop at three in the morning, many of these conversations carried fantastic weight with them at the time we talked, but that weight quickly dissipated and would be gone by the morning. The difference was that we had many years of life experience between the years of our youth and the time we were living in the now. We may not have been old, but we were certainly older, and at least a little bit wiser, than we had been.

It was during one of these conversations that I was introduced to a phrase I had never heard before but instantly made sense to me, and has become almost a yardstick as to how I view my life. We were talking about the people we had met since we'd been on the island (I had only been there about six months longer than they had) and how different they all were. To be fair, I didn't think that, at an island outpost one hundred plus miles from the mainland sitting in the middle of a tropical sea, I was going to come across a slice of Middle America. It is a certain type of person who can live and work and exist and thrive in such an environment. What made it possible to do that, they told me, was to meet a certain type of person.

An O.P.L.U., to be exact.

O.P.L.U. stands for Other Person Like Us. A kindred spirit, a fellow traveler on the same pilgrimage, someone whose values and goals and ideals lie in the same ballpark as yours. The idea of this is obviously nothing new. Look at the people who are part of your life. The more choice you have about them being there, the more like you, and you like them, they probably are. Your spouse most certainly should be an O.P.L.U. After all, you two chose each other. People at work probably not so much. Just because you work at the same place doesn't mean you have that much to share. Everyone else probably falls somewhere in between. This concept, as obvious as it might be, should never be overlooked.

These two are my friends for countless reasons, reasons that will always make them my friends. But I find myself wondering if they ever would have become my friends if I had been a bartender in, say, New York and not Key West. Would we have recognized in each other the elements that made us bond and become so close, or, in an environment where it wasn't so obvious, would that opportunity have slipped away? There is absolutely no doubt in my mind that they helped to save me from myself, and their presence in my life is as important as anyone else, especially at a time when I needed all the help in the world. These were the room mates I had when I found rock bottom. These were the people who, even though we shared many crazy exploits on the island, were the ones to help introduce me to the fact that I was no longer living the life I wanted to be. They had a very real connection to the outside world through their jobs, and their presence at that time in that place reminded me of all that I had let myself forget.

This is not to say that, as you begin a journey of change in your life, that you need to eliminate everyone else from your life and only look for people going through exactly what you are. First of all, you ain't going to find anyone like that, and secondly, and way more importantly, the people in your life all have wonderful stuff to help you. I probably have more differences than similarities with this couple I've been talking about, but it is not the differences that I concern myself with. Likewise, when I think of two of my best friends, I recognize that even though I have so much in common with both of them, they have very little in common with each other. That doesn't mean I should eliminate one or the other from my life. Most people already in your life offer you little things that help nurture and support you. It is simply to help build on that support that as you grow there will be new people that you will meet. Whether it is an active search you go on, finding social clubs and support networks, or a more passive approach, like simply being aware when they walk into your workplace, the truth is they are out there, needing you just like you need them, and together with them, you can each grow farther than you imagined.

Looking down the rabbit hole

This will probably be the most serious part of the book. Now, if you just read that and your first thought was along the lines of "Hasn't the whole book been serious?" then we need to have an important discussion about the difference between serious and important.

This book is important. Everything in the book is important, or at least as important as you want it to be. If nothing else, it will at least be important in that it helped steer the path you were on. Even if there wasn't much from this book you could pull, you learned where to start looking for the stuff you needed. That's important. But if you go back, you'll notice that very rarely was I serious about all the stuff that is so important, and that's the difference. You don't have to be serious when talking about something important and it doesn't have to be something important that you have to be serious about. A wedding is about as important an event as a person can have in their lives, but if your friends are anything like mine, they tend to be some of the most light-hearted, fun and uplifting experiences people have together. Weekly meetings at your job may not be nearly as important as your boss thinks they are, but try not being serious during one, and that meeting will go on twice as long as you want it to. There is a very important difference. The words do not have to be used together, but sometimes they certainly can be. This is one of those times. This chapter is just as important as the rest. It just also happens to be serious.

I used to think I knew what depression was. I thought it was like any other emotion, one you could just deal with and accept and move on from. I used to always give myself one day to deal with anything whether it was good or bad and then move on. But depression is something more than just being upset or being angry or sad. It is something that consumes you without concern and now I can't begin to understand it. The euphoria I felt when I moved home is gone and I'm back to where I had been, not thinking my life was anything more than a shit heap. I wish I could just will myself out of it, but I don't know that I can anymore.

Pretty uplifting thought, huh? I wrote that quite some time ago. (The joy of the computer is that you can keep all the old stuff and see where your thought process was.) When I tell you that I am writing this as I go through the journey, I ain't just whistling Dixie. This work is as much for me as it is for you. That paragraph was far from the most depressing stuff on my hard drive. There was stuff that I was dealing with that I couldn't begin to get a handle on it, but only through digging into it and working at it could I come to terms with it and move on. But first, I had to accept it.

I would go to parties full of people who were my friends and have to leave in less than an hour because my anxiety would be too much. These were not parties full of complete strangers that I'd be dragged to by a friend with the false promise "Come on, it'll be great." These were people I have known for a long time, hosted by friends I had known even longer. You would think that there could not be a more inviting, comforting place to be. You'd be right, but you'd also be forgetting one thing.

These were the same people I felt I had let down. These were the same people I was convinced that could see right through me and know that I was a failure. I would go to these parties and I wouldn't see all of my friends. All I would see was the two thousand pound elephant in the corner that was named "Failure". I knew that was his name because I could see it painted all over his body. Everywhere I looked he was there to remind me that I had failed at being the person I wanted to be, and knowing that governed everything I did. I couldn't join in conversations because I was convinced I would say the wrong thing. I couldn't sit down next to people because I was sure they didn't want me there. I couldn't eat the food because it wasn't there for me. It was only there for the successful people. This was what I lived with all the time, and I couldn't figure out why.

When I had been younger, and more in touch with my dreams and where I wanted to be headed in this world, I viewed depression not as a life crippling disease, but merely an inconvenience that could be willed away. I had a tried and true method in my life for dealing with anything, either good or bad. I would give myself one day to wallow in it, and then I would move on. If something good happened, like getting cast in a play, or scoring well in class, something of an achievement, I would give myself one day to celebrate, and then I would move on. Yes it had been a good thing, but life hadn't come to a screeching halt. It's like what Kevin Costner says to Tim Robbins in "Bull Durham" when Tim's character is proud of the inning he threw and wants to bask in the moment. "The moment's passed. Move on." Likewise, when something bad happened that brought me down, I would give myself one day to be as sad and upset as I wanted to be, and then the next day, I would move on. I knew nothing was going to get better if I didn't make it better. I gave myself a day to be with my feelings, and then I let them go.

That was what I used to think depression was: feeling bad about something. Letting something bad that happened to you weigh you down. To me it was no different then sad or upset, and I honestly couldn't understand how people could claim to be depressed. Just get over it, I thought. If I can, so could you. How hard can it be?

I didn't know depression. I didn't know what it felt like to want to turn on the shower, climb in there, and want to stay there for the next six hours. I didn't know what it was like to lay in bed until the last possible minute, and the moment you got out you started counting the minutes until you could climb back in there. I didn't know what it was like to feel actual fear every time the phone rang because you didn't know how to talk to people anymore, not when the only thing you thought they'd want to talk about was what a failure you were. I didn't know what it was like to look in the mirror and not recognize the person staring back at you because there was no way this ugly, washed up, beaten down person could possibly have been you, only to start crying because you finally realize it couldn't be anyone but you, and you couldn't remember how you had gotten there and, worse, you didn't know how or if you'd ever get back.

That's depression. And that's why this is the most serious part of this book.

Only one person knows why you're here, and that's you. So you need to ask yourself a direct question and give yourself an honest answer. Where are you at emotionally in your life right now?

The reason I ask is crucial.

One of the things that finally helped me move forward towards being more positive in my life and heal my depression was when I realized I was doing so much to try to mask what was going on inside of me. Trying to create relationships just so I'd be in one and not have to face what I was up against. Being the life of the party so much so that the next day I couldn't remember the party, just so I wouldn't remember everything else. Pouring all of my energy and focus into a job I didn't care about just so it would consume my life and give me less time to address the root problems of my life. And when none of those things could happen, I would take the hour long showers and spend all day in bed, just waiting until the next distraction came around. That leads to the next question:

Are you reading this because you are ready for this to help heal your life and make you better, or because it's just the latest in a long list of band aids you've been trying on?

In other words, am I catching you on the way up, or the way down?

Once again, only you can answer that question, and you need to do it honestly, because if the answer is that you're on your way down, that you've been grasping at straws for the last several weeks or months, or maybe even years, hoping to find something that just makes you feel good and forget about all your problems, then I'm going to give you some stone cold advice that you need to hear.

Put down the book, pick up the phone and call somebody. Not just any somebody, but somebody who is trained to help you. Call a therapist, a shrink, your pastor, the help line at the local hospital, somebody who has the skills to help you deal with and work through your problems and not just simply forget them. Call them, and tell them what you just told yourself, about where you are at emotionally in your life, how you've been trying so many other things but nothing's been working, and you feel like you're on the way down. There is no shame in recognizing that there are problems bigger than what you can handle, and even bigger than what you can realize. The first time I went to see my shrink, the session was all about me giving my life story. Every so often he kept asking me questions about acting and if I was doing any or how it made me feel, and I found myself getting confused, wondering if he was even listening to me, because I knew my problems had nothing to do with acting and everything to do with what was going on now in my life. It was only later that I realized it was the frustrations of not living out those dreams and losing touch of that energy and passion I had had all those years ago that was at the root of what I was up against. At the time, the only thing I could see was that my life sucked, I was a failure and all I wanted to do was sleep.

I can help you. My experiences can serve as lessons for you to learn by. My achievements can be an ideal for you to think about as you move forward on your own path. My success can be an inspiration. But in the end, I'm just a guy who wrote a book. There is a finite amount you can get from me. Outside of rereading this book and gleaning new information from it, something you might have missed the first time, there's nothing more I'm offering you. Call someone who's there, someone who has the time, the place and most importantly the ability to be there for you.

And not to be as my friend says a "Dougie Downer", but every so often I'll get in the shower, and it'll be just the right temperature and I'll be just tired enough that I'll find myself thinking "Man, I could stay here all day." What gets me out is the knowledge that if I did that, then there would be so many wonderful things I wouldn't get to do that day. Once upon a time I didn't realize that, but now I do.

You can too.

Breathe

I've tried really hard not to give specific instruction as to what you should be doing to make your life better. I truly believe that everything you learn is useless until you go out and do it on your own, and all that I can offer a person is the comfort and support of "Hey, I've been where you are, I've gotten through it and so can you." It's like anything else. You can read all you want about being a brain surgeon (or a bowler), but until you actually go out and put it in practice, you never know if you have actually learned it. Well, now it's time to know, and so it's time for me to tell you what to do.

Breathe.

I know what you're thinking. That you've wasted all this time and money, and this is the big secret? Breathing is what is going to make you a better, more positive person? Well, yes and no. The "No" part is that it is not just breathing that will make you a better person. The "Yes" part is that it is the keystone to all that comes after it.

Breathing is (obviously) something we don't have to think about. Our body knows to do it naturally. Involuntary muscle action they call it. Diaphragm collapses, air comes in. Diaphragm expands, air goes out. This happens, offhand, a bajillion-zillion times in our lives. It happens so effortlessly that we don't even pay attention to it. And yet it is the most important thing that keeps us alive.

Think about it. How long can you go without food or water? People routinely fast for a day at a time. Some go even longer than that. If you had to, you could go twenty four hours without eating or drinking. It wouldn't be pleasant, but it could be done. Now, try going twenty four *minutes* without breathing. Go ahead. I'll wait.

Yeah, I didn't think so either. Breath is life itself. A baby is born and what's the first thing they do? Smack its ass and make sure it's breathing. And that is what anyone who wants to grow needs to do. Smack themselves and make sure they are truly breathing.

If you are still following the directions from the second part of the introduction, you are sitting somewhere comfortable as you read this. What I want you to do is finish reading this paragraph and then do what it says. Put the book down, preferably not on your lap or in contact with your body. Then close your eyes and put your hands on your stomach. I want you to take some deep breaths, nine in all, really concentrating on filling yourself with the breath, and then feeling it all escape as you exhale. Try not to think about anything else. If you're like most people, you're going to feel silly and stupid and a little self conscious, but just let all that go. It's just you and me here. So give it a shot.

How was it? If you managed to not get your mind bogged down in judging and commenting on what you were doing, and really just concentrated on breathing in and out, filling your body with life itself, you probably found yourself breathing deeper than you normally do. With it, you probably felt a sense of calm. You relaxed just a little bit more than normal, and maybe even when you opened your eyes and picked the book back up, you found yourself moving just a little bit slower, but with a more definite purpose. Even in reading this, you find yourself more in tune with it, and that there are less distractions going on inside your head, as you think about why you're doing this, what you're getting out of this, and where you're going to go for dinner tonight. And if you're like most people, you were already starting to think about other stuff like that even before I mentioned it. But that's normal. You are very subtly and yet very profoundly changing the way you live your life. It is going to take a lot of very tiny steps.

Progress on anything like this is not measured in quick turn around times. It took me nine months before I even began to feel that I had changed and been able to see a difference between where I was when I started and where I had gotten to. And that's just the beginning. I'm sure I've got several years to go before the changes I work on every day (and I do mean every day) become second nature to who I am and they become an inherent part of me. When thinking about it in terms like that, it's hard not to get discouraged, but you need to keep reminding yourself that everyday you are doing something that is a little better for you than the day before. And that is where taking the time to concentrate on just your breathing is important.

Every day when you get up, yawn, stretch, scratch, burp, do

whatever you do when you take your body from asleep to awake. Then, when you have gotten through all that and gotten over the inevitable "I wanna be back in bed" find a nice quiet place to be where you can sit comfortably and just spend a couple of minutes with your breath. Feel it flow into every part of your body. Imagine it running through your arms and legs and into your fingers and toes. Imagine that when you are breathing in, you are pulling in pure energy, and when you breathe out you are giving away all your tension and anxiety, and allowing yourself to be open to this brand new day and all its possibilities. And when your mind starts to wander (and it will, so don't start beating yourself up because you are doing something wrong) lead it to where it needs to be and what your next step is. Are you having trouble accepting yourself? Are you still not able to let go of expectations? Whatever it is, as you concentrate on your breath filling and empowering you, let that breath give you the strength to move forward, to accept yourself, to let go of expectation, to be a little bit more today than you were yesterday the person you know yourself to be.

Spend a few minutes with that, and then go on with your day, being sure to remember what that felt like and taking the time through the course of the day to check back in with it. Doesn't have to be much, just the few seconds waiting for the elevator, or thirty seconds right when you come back for lunch. (Try not to do it when your boss is talking to you, though. They may not appreciate not having your full attention.) Just enough so that is slowly and truly becomes part of who you are.

Soon you will notice that you don't think about it anymore, that whatever was holding you up at first no longer comes to mind. And just like that, you have moved that much closer to being a complete person. Like I said, it is a process that takes a long time; indeed, you could say it takes a lifetime, because there will always be something more you can learn about living a better, more positive life. I think about it in relation to my weight loss issues. It took me a long time to get fat, it's going to take me a long time to get thin. The difference is that I wasn't paying attention to when I was getting fat, so I didn't notice how long it took. But now that I am working to lose weight and get in better shape, I am that much more aware of the time passing (or more accurately, not passing as fast as I want it to) and more apt to let it frustrate me. You just have to trust that, if you make the effort, the results will come, and your patience will be rewarded.

As a perfect example of what it takes to make this happen, I am going to put my trust in you right now. There is one more chapter in this book. I don't want you to read it yet. I want you to put a book mark in, put the book down, and walk away from it for seven days. In that time that you are gone, I want you to wake every morning and take the time to focus your breath and your energy, and I want you to be sure to check in with it during the course of the day. The other thing I want you to do is think about all that I've talked about and start to really ask yourself where is it in your life you want to be going. I want you to find an adjective that best describes it. It's already accepted that you want to be more positive. You have to be if you want to change your life. But think of the word that would fill in this sentence: I want to be a _____ person.

Loving? Compassionate? Humorous? Think about what brought you to this book in the first place, and what one word could describe that best. And don't worry; there is no right or wrong answer. Just let it drift through mind during the quiet moments.

But whatever you do, don't forget to come back to this in seven days. You've done a lot of learning, and you're almost done. I'd hate to see you fall short now.

Besides, I get lonely.

And now?

Welcome back. Did you make it? It's all right if you didn't. Like I said there is no wrong or right answers in any of this, it's all about making the decisions and engaging the action. Truth is I'd be surprised if you went the whole seven days. In fact, if you're like most people, had you tried to go the full time, you might not have come back at all. Here's why:

Whenever a person begins to examine their life, the first emotions that tend to come up are going to be negative ones. It is simply a process of taking these feelings from the subconscious to the conscious. You wouldn't be working on changing your life if you didn't feel inside of you that there was something lacking. Well, now you're actively addressing that situation, and it moves to the forefront of your mind. It becomes something you now are dealing with all the time, in what may seem like the oddest of situations. "I don't know if I should get the chicken or the beef, because I think there's something wrong with me emotionally." After a while this obviously becomes frustrating, and you find yourself faced with three choices:

1) See how much longer you can make it.
2) Realize it's gotten to be too much and you need to get some guidance or help with it.
3) Quit.

If you chose the first option and made it the full seven days, that's awesome. But if you chose option two, that's still awesome, because you recognize that there is still work to be done and you want to do it. You are still committed to moving forward, to becoming a more positive person and letting this positivity color how you live your life. (And if you chose option three, it doesn't much matter what I think about you, because you're not reading this.)

So, now what? That's what you're probably asking yourself. The book is finished, now what do I do? The short answer is something. Anything. Just as long as it's something different. It may be a cliché but it's true: If you're going to keep doing the same thing, you're going to keep getting the same results. (On a side note, they say the definition of insanity is doing the same thing over and over and expecting different results. Just something to think about.) What you need to remember though is that doing it once isn't enough. You can't do it once, and then sit back and expect (See? There's that forbidden word again) things to suddenly be different. It is a new life you are embarking on, one that must be respected every day. You may do the same new thing every day for a week and not feel anything different other than stupid for trying something new. Remember the bowling story? One week of practicing will not get anyone ready for the PBA tour. Stay with it, believe in it, believe in yourself, knowing that you are doing something that is good, that is better than you have been, and you will start to feel it, until it becomes an organic part of who you are.

One thing that I promised a long time earlier in the book to bring up was the fact that I would never say anything is complete. I said the book is finished, but I didn't say it was complete. Truth be told I could very easily continue to add to this for the rest of my life, as new insights become apparent and I continue to grow and change. There is no ever "complete". Life is not a work of fiction created to have a beginning, middle and end. While there are certainly chapters in our lives that have definitive endpoints (starting a new job, ending a relationship) those are not the beginning and ends of our lives. We were before they started, we will be after they are over.

In a reissue of the novel _The Stand_, Stephen King writes about discussing the book with his readers and people asking him what has become of the characters "as if they existed somewhere and sent me letters, telling me of their lives." Characters in a work of fiction have a finite lifespan, tied directly into the plot of their story. When the plot is resolved, so is their existence. The only plot we have to live out is that of our own lives, lives that are constantly in flux and presenting us with ever-changing new challenges. Overcoming a challenge does not award us the opportunity to be static the rest of our lives. A new day comes tomorrow, and life continues and we continue with it, finding out more truths about ourselves and learning how to live better, richer, fuller lives.

I longed to be that nineteen year old kid again, to the point that I never let that kid grow up. I have struggled with that truth for many years. One look at my list of addresses will show you that. I have never taken the time to confront the reality of growing up. Whenever things got too tough, or too serious, or too real, I have simply moved on, usually with very little thought about what was going to happen next, or in some cases even where I was going. And as I did, I made a very small mistake that had very large consequences. I kept latching on to who I had been at that point in my life. To me, that had been the high point of my life. I was successful at what I was doing, I was surrounded by more friends than I had ever thought I had, I had a dream that I found the courage to follow. I was invincible. Before college even ended for me though, I fell away from that courage. Doubt and fear crept into my mind, and I panicked that I wouldn't be able to continue to live with that vitality, that I wouldn't be able to still have that strength and personality. I lost faith in myself and who I was and what I had learned. Instead of growing from that point, I locked down on that point, telling myself "If this is when I was happiest and most successful, then this is where I should live my life from." The difference being instead of learning from that 19 year old and growing from there, I wanted to remain that 19 year old, frozen in time. Without even thinking about it, I was not doing what I wanted. I was doing what I could.

Now I know the difference. Now I am doing what I want, and I know that it can be anything. I am living my life again, not anyone else's. And I don't simply know that I could do anything that I want. I feel it. I feel it in the blood that flows through my veins; I feel it in my bones when I wake up in the morning. I feel it in every breath I take. Am I interested in pursuing those dreams that fueled that nineteen year old kid again? Right now "no". Right now I'm still more interested in finding out more about me again. I am still putting back some of the pieces I've lost over the years. (Kinda feel like the Six Million Dollar Man a little bit. I can make myself faster, stronger, better. Now I just need that cool whoosh-whooosh-whooosh sound effect he had every time he ran.) Maybe some point in the future I'll get back to it, ready to give it the effort, respect and dedication it deserves. Or maybe I'll learn so much about myself that I'll learn I don't need those dreams anymore.

That's me. What about you? Well, I told you I was going to

have one last lesson for you, something for you to do that, if nothing else, will give you a jumping off point for the day. Hopefully you've gotten into the habit of stopping every morning and centering your breath, and keeping that with you as you go through the day. We're going to add one simple but very powerful step to it. I want you to do it now, and then I want you to do it every morning, after your little breathing exercise. If you are like most people, at some point first thing in the morning you end up in the bathroom. When you're there, stand in front of the mirror, feet shoulder width apart and hands by your side. Take some time to look in the mirror and really see yourself.

Now, did you pick out that adjective like I told you to? Good. You're going to slip it into the following sentence:

"I am a positive _____ person."

Some of you are laughing, some of you are scratching your head and some of you are saying "This guy's full of crap." Fine. Prove me wrong. Try it a few times. Say it silently the first time. (You'll probably want to anyway because you're paranoid someone else who lives in the house is going to hear you and say "Honey, what are you doing?") But say it and mean it. Really hear the words. Say it again, this time whispering it, but being sure to really enunciate each word. Don't blow this off and try to race through it. Really hear what you are saying. Let the words sink into you and become part of who you are.

Say it again, this time a little slower.

Say it again, this time a little louder.

And again, even louder this time.

Again, louder and slower.

Funny thing starts to happen if you let go and trust in it. You feel it in your body. You feel an energy start to run through you. Your nose probably even starts to tingle. You know why? Because you probably forgot to keep breathing. So take a deep breath, and say it again.

"I am a positive _____ person."

Every day I start my life with "I am a positive creative person." And I don't stop until I feel it. And not just me thinking about it and recognizing it, but until I feel invincible, powerful, and, most importantly, creative and positive.

There is an energy, a presence inside all of us, that we lose contact with over the years. We all have gifts. We just don't always remember that they are there. Today, as this chapter literally ends, a new chapter begins figuratively in your life. Today you begin finding your gifts, the gifts of who you are as a person, of how to reawaken that person, to become a whole person again, to become a person you are proud of, the person you know yourself to be, and ultimately to share that new person and help others find their own gifts. We are all our own angels here on Earth, beautiful creatures full of power and light and promise for the better life we want to be living.

The final truth

      As I prepare this to send to the publisher (seriously, I'm sending it out this week) there is one more thing I feel I need to share. Those of you who know me already know this, and those of you who don't probably found out by reading my bio. You see, I do in fact live back in Key West. After reading the central part of this book, you might be thinking I'm either a fraud or an idiot (or even a fraudulent idiot) but the simple truth is a lot has gone down between then and now. When I came here the last time, it was as rash a decision as I've ever made, and I was still as lost in my life as I have ever been. Now, it was a willful, well thought out decision, one that I came to after much internal debate and, as written about, after a long time with a therapist. Now I am comfortable with who I am and why I am here. Yes, I'm sure that part of the motivation in moving back was to prove something to myself and no, I do not believe I am done growing or changing, but in a very real sense I feel as if I have retired from my old life, my lost life, and down here I have begun to live a new life, the life I feel like I should have been living all along. This does not mean I reject my old life; my friends are still my friends and I probably love and appreciate them more now than I have in the past, if for no other reason I am more aware of who I am and what my dreams and goals are than I have been for a very long time. Will I stay here forever? I don't know. I can say that the thought of spending winters back in the cold does not hold much interest for me anymore, but I do not know what the future holds and I cannot pretend to even guess. My life is here and now, and the best I can do is make the best of every day as it comes to me.

      I hope you do the same.

Jack Terry
Key West
December 30th, 2011

About the author

Jack Terry was born and raised in Plainville, Connecticut. Upon graduation, he attended New York University. Armed with a fresh (and reasonably impractical) B.F.A. in Drama, he followed a somewhat family tradition by moving to San Francisco. Between now and then his wandering feet have taken him back to Connecticut and New York a couple of times, as well as Los Angeles, Milwaukee and Oxford, Pennsylvania, where he spent a year watching his nephews slowly grow taller than he is, before eventually returning to Key West. His first book, the novel *"Chasing Ghosts"*, was published in 2010. When not home writing or tending bar, he can most commonly be found wherever there is warm sun, hot sand, cool drinks and good music. For more information and to purchase his books, go to his website:

www.popcornjackterry.com

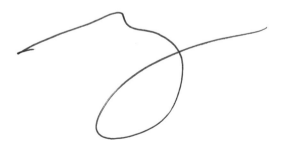

Made in the USA
Charleston, SC
24 April 2012